From Ellie's Kitchen To Yours

Be sure to visit
www.EllieDeaner.com
for more recipes.

From Ellie's Kitchen To Yours

Ellie Deaner

Cover Photograph
Jonathan N. Deaner

Denell Press
Framingham, Massachusetts

FROM ELLIE'S KITCHEN TO YOURS.

Copyright© 1991 by Ellie Deaner

All right reserved. Printed in the United States of America. No part of this book may be used or reproduced in any manner whatsoever without written permission except in the case of brief quotations embodied in critical articles and reviews.

For information:
Denell Press
34 Crestwood Dr
Framingham, Massachusetts 01701

FIRST PRINTING – November 1991
SECOND PRINTING – March 1993
THIRD PRINTING – June 1998
FOURTH PRINTING – March 1999
FIFTH PRINTING – February 2001
SIXTH PRINTING – September 2002
SEVENTH PRINTING – March 2008

ISBN 0-9631177-7-7

Contents

Introduction

I have always loved food and have been genuinely interested in its taste, preparation and presentation. This can probably be attributed to the fact that I was brought up in a family of European heritage in which cooking and baking played a very important role. In fact, my parents had a home-based specialty baking business so the whole family was totally involved in it.

Some of my fondest childhood memories are the times I spent in the kitchen with my mother and grandmother, who both brought over many wonderful recipes from Europe. The appreciation of all their good tasting and attractively presented food strongly influenced me, as well as encouraged me, to experiment in my own kitchen.

When I made the transition from bride to mother, I voraciously read cookbooks, tried new recipes and attended as many cooking classes as possible. After a few years, I was considered the neighborhood cooking expert and friends began calling me for recipes, advice and asking me to teach them how to cook and bake. Finally, one of my closest friends encouraged me to begin teaching cooking. My first class was held at a local YWCA. When the series was over, my students asked me to teach additional classes. This gave me the impetus to establish a cooking school in my home. Then I was asked to write a food column for a local newspaper, give demonstrations for organizations and lunchtime seminars for corporations. At that point my cooking career was well on its way.

When I began teaching cooking in 1976, people were entertaining and wanted "fancy" and "gourmet" menus for their dinner parties. Fewer women were working then and therefore had more time to spend in the kitchen. Now, in the 1990s, life is more hectic and complex so most people have much less time for cooking and baking. However, they still want to serve their families and friends meals that are nutritious, quick and easy to prepare and that can be made partially or completely in advance. People also want to use ingredients that are reasonably priced and available in the local supermarket. When selecting the recipes for my book, I tried to keep these factors in mind.

This book would not have been possible without the continuous support of my parents, sister, good friends and cooking students. They have all generously shared recipes with me, some of which appear in this book, allowed me to test countless recipes and menus on them and helped to proofread much of this book. Most importantly, I thank my wonderful husband and partner in the production and publishing of this book. I am also indebted to my three sons who have constantly had to sample new recipes. My family has given unlimited support, love, patience and time to me and this project. I love them all very much for that.

Using this Book

The following conventions are used throughout this book.

Fats: Many recipes contain a choice of butter, margarine or oil, as well as a range of amounts, so that individuals limiting their fat intake can choose the kind and amount of fat they want to use.

Freshly ground black pepper: Freshly ground pepper is tastier than that from a spice jar. Therefore, if you have a pepper mill, it is best to use it.

Fresh herbs: Whenever possible, use fresh herbs such as parsley, dill, chives, etc. (see Ingredients and Substitutions).

Preheating oven: It is assumed that the oven is preheated to the baking temperature, unless otherwise specified.

Salt, to taste: Many people limit their salt and/or sodium intake so they can season food according to their own taste and dietary restrictions.

Serving size: Portion sizes are generally not given because
• it depends on what else is being served
• people's appetites vary greatly
• all recipes may be halved, doubled or tripled

Helpful Equipment

The equipment listed below can be helpful in reducing your time in the kitchen.

Colander: to drain pasta, fruits and vegetables

Cutting board: to protect your counter tops

Decorating knife: to zigzag edges of peppers, oranges, lemons, melons etc. This is also known as a V-cut knife.

Electric mixer: to make cakes, cookies and breads

Food processor: to grate cheese, carrots, potatoes, mix salad dressings, spreads and pie dough, to chop vegetables and herbs, and to puree soups, dips and fruits. The steel blade of the processor is what is used, unless otherwise specified.

Garlic press: to mince garlic

Goosefeather brush: to brush egg, butter, milk etc. on cookie, pie, cake, bread, or any delicate dough

Grapefruit knife: to section grapefruit, cut pineapple, hollow-out loaves of bread and to aid in many garnishing tasks

Knives: use good quality cutlery for all cooking tasks. The most important size knives are a 3 to 4-inch paring, a 6-inch utility, 8-inch chef's, 10-inch slicer and a bread knife. A good sharpening steel for the knives is a must.

Lemon juicer or reamer: to make fresh lemon juice

Lemon stripper: to remove long strips of rind from lemons, limes and oranges for recipes calling for large pieces of rind, to make lemon twists for beverages, to make garnishes with cucumbers, oranges, lemons and mushrooms

Lemon zester: to remove the rind from lemons, limes and oranges without the bitter pith

Measuring spoons and cups: to ensure accuracy

Meat pounder: to pound chicken, turkey or veal cutlets

Microwave oven: to heat leftovers, defrost food quickly, cook fruits, vegetables and fish, melt butter and chocolate, make puddings and sauces, etc. Unless otherwise specified, recipes in this book that refer to the microwave use high, or full power (650-700 watts).

Nutmeg grater: to grind fresh nutmeg

Pepper mill: to grind fresh pepper

Rubber scraper: to clean bowls and mixers

Salad spinner: to dry salad greens, herbs, berries and grapes

Scissors: to use for many kitchen tasks

Timer: to accurately time cooking and baking

Vegetable steamer: to steam (instead of boil) vegetables on top of the stove

V-cut knife: see decorating knife

Whisk: to whip egg whites and cream, to mix ingredients and to aid in making sauces

Wok: a metal cooking pan with a convex bottom, used for stir-frying, deep-frying, braising and steaming

Wooden spoons: to stir ingredients on top of the stove

Ingredients and Substitutions

This is a list of the basic ingredients, as well as their substitutions, most commonly used in this book. They are available in most supermarkets.

Butter or margarine: Most recipes offer you a choice, although a few specifically tell you that butter or half butter and half margarine are preferred, for taste.

Cheese: You can substitute low fat varieties for many kinds of cheese.

Cottage cheese: Substitute low fat or nonfat cottage for regular cottage cheese.

Cream: May be referred to in the book as "all purpose", "medium" or "whipping". All of these will make whipped cream, but contain less butterfat than heavy cream. To reduce fat, you can often substitute evaporated skim milk for cream, if the cream does not need to be whipped.

Dill: Use fresh or frozen rather than dried, if possible.

Eggs: Always use large, unless stated otherwise.

Flour: Always use unbleached and unsifted, unless otherwise specified.

Garlic: Keep bulbs of fresh garlic at room temperature. Use a garlic press, sharp knife or food processor to mince.

Lemon juice: Always use fresh. To get the most juice from a lemon, let it sit at room temperature for at least 30 minutes.

Mayonnaise: You can substitute fat free, low calorie or cholesterol free for regular mayonnaise.

Nonstick cooking spray: Use to reduce fat and save time.

Nutmeg: Grind in a nutmeg grater for best flavor.

Oil: Physicians and dieticians currently recommend olive and canola oils as being the lowest in saturated fat. Peanut and sesame oils are often used in oriental recipes.

Parmesan cheese: Use freshly ground Parmesan cheese whenever possible.

Parsley: Use fresh parsley if possible. As with all fresh herbs, wash and dry in a salad spinner. Mince with a sharp chef's knife or food processor. If not using immediately, place in a plastic container or bags and freeze. To keep fresh parsley sprigs for garnish, wash and spin dry and wrap them in a paper towel. Place in a plastic bag and refrigerate for up to 10 days. Use the same method for fresh dill, basil, mint, oregano, etc.

Pasta: Use fresh or dried.

Pepper: Grind black or white peppercorns in a pepper mill for best flavor

Rind: Use a lemon zester to remove the fresh rind (outer skin) from lemons, limes, oranges and grapefruits.

Salt: Reduce as much as possible in cooking and baking.

Sour cream: You can often replace sour cream with a reduced fat sour cream or with low fat or nonfat yogurt.

Soy sauce: Substitue low sodium soy sauce for regular soy sauce.

Whole milk: You can usually substitute low fat or skim milk for whole milk.

Yeast: Find in the dairy section of supermarkets.

Yogurt: Use nonfat instead of low fat. You can often substitute yogurt for buttermilk, sour milk or sour cream.

Hors d'oeuvres and Beverages

CHEESE POCKET TOPPER

1 pt mayonnaise
1 lb Swiss cheese, shredded
¼ C fresh parsley, finely chopped
½ C Parmesan cheese, or to taste

1 onion, finely chopped
Garlic powder, to taste
2 9 oz pkgs pita bread

Combine all ingredients except pita bread. Split and cut pita bread into triangles. Spread cheese mixture on bread and broil until cheese melts and gets bubbly and golden.

Hint: This is one of the all time best and easiest recipes. It was created by one of my favorite cooking students. It makes a tremendous hit at parties, as well as with my own family, as a snack. The mixture may be made a few days in advance and kept in a jar in the refrigerator. This recipe uses a large quantity of triangles so you may want to cut it in half. It's good to have on hand if you have guests and suddenly want to make a snack. Just spread the mixture on pita bread or English muffins and broil.

SCALLOPS WRAPPED IN BACON

1 lb sea scallops
½ C teriyaki sauce

1 lb bacon

Wash and drain scallops. Cut large ones in half. Marinate in teriyaki sauce for several hours or overnight. Wrap one-third to one-half strip of bacon around scallop and secure with a toothpick. Bake at 425°, or broil until bacon is crisp, turning until evenly cooked.

Yield: approximately 40

Hint: You can prepare these a few hours in advance and bake them when needed.

1

BAKED SALAMI

12 oz kosher salami that is shaped like a bullet

Remove all wrappings around salami. Wrap in foil. Bake at 250° for 2 hours. Remove foil and serve with party rye bread and a variety of mustards.

Hint: This is one of the easiest recipes imaginable. It's nice for a cocktail or Superbowl party. You may substitute bologna for salami.

HONEY MUSTARD PINWHEELS

1 pkg Pepperidge Farm Puff Pastry Sheets

Honey mustard
1 egg, beaten with 1 tsp water

Remove dough from freezer and defrost at room temperature for one hour or in refrigerator for several hours. Unfold dough and roll on a lightly floured surface to an 11"x14" rectangle. Spread with enough Honey mustard to coat the dough. Starting at long edge, roll up pastry jellyroll fashion. Cut pastry into ¼ to ⅜-inch slices. Turn slices onto their sides and brush with egg mixture. Place on parchment-lined cookie sheets about 1½ inches apart. Bake at 375° for 10 to 13 minutes, or until pastry is golden. Serve hot.

Yield: 5 to 6 dozen pinwheels

VARIATION:

PESTO PINWHEELS

1 pkg Pepperidge Farm Puff Pastry Sheets
⅔ C pesto sauce (store bought or homemade)
1 C Parmesan cheese, freshly grated

Spread pesto on dough. Sprinkle with cheese and roll up, as above.

Yield: 5 to 6 dozen pinwheels

Hint: If there are leftover pinwheels, keep them in a tin and serve at room temperature or reheat at 350° for about 5 minutes. These pinwheels may also be frozen before baking by wrapping filled, unsliced pastry logs tightly in plastic wrap and freezing for several hours or up to a few months. Remove logs 15 minutes before baking. Slice and bake as directed above.

CHEDDAR CHEESE PUFF

1 pkg Pepperidge Farm
Puff Pastry Sheets
8 oz Cheddar cheese, shredded

Dash paprika
1 egg white, beaten
1 T sesame seeds

Remove dough from freezer and defrost at room temperature for 1 hour or in refrigerator for several hours. Open package and roll out each of the two sheets of dough until they are about 2 to 3 inches larger than before being rolled. Sprinkle cheese in a circle in the center of one sheet of dough. Sprinkle with paprika. Place other piece of dough directly on top. Cut off corners of dough so that it may be shaped into a circle. Press edges of dough together all over so that cheese will not leak out when baked. Flute edges of dough as you would a pie crust or press edges together with the tines of a fork. Make air vents in pastry using the tip of a knife or tines of a fork. Brush with egg white and sprinkle with sesame seeds. Bake at 350° for 20 to 25 minutes or until golden. Allow to cool for 10 minutes before cutting into wedges.

Hint: You may assemble this up to 2 days in advance, then refrigerate and bake when needed. Brush with egg white just before baking. Shredded cheese such as Swiss, Fontina, Monterey Jack or a one pound round of Brie may be substituted for the Cheddar. Also, the corners of the dough that get removed when shaping into a circle may be cut into designs and placed as decoration on top of puff after it has been brushed with egg white. Then brush design with egg white also. If you don't want to use these scraps of dough to decorate your puff, you may sprinkle them with sugar and cinnamon or Parmesan cheese, bake at 350° for 10 to 15 minutes, and eat as a snack!

SPINACH SQUARES

2 10 oz pkgs frozen chopped spinach,
    thawed, squeezed and drained
3½ T butter or margarine, melted
3 eggs
1 C milk

1 tsp baking powder
1 T onion, finely chopped
1 C flour
½ tsp salt, or to taste
1 lb sharp Cheddar cheese, grated

Melt butter or margarine in a 9"x13" pan. Combine all remaining ingredients except spinach. Mix well. Then add spinach. Pour into pan containing melted butter or margarine. Bake at 350° for 35 minutes. Cool 45 minutes before cutting.

Hint: This recipe may be made in advance and refrigerated or frozen. Cut into bite-size pieces to serve as hors d'oeuvres or into larger pieces to serve as a side dish with a meal or as part of a dinner buffet.

3

CHINESE EGG ROLLS

FILLING:

½ lb raw shrimp, chopped
½ lb ground pork
1 C scallions, chopped
4 C Chinese cabbage, shredded
1 C carrots, shredded
1 C bean sprouts

2 T canola or peanut oil, divided
¼ tsp pepper
¼ tsp ground ginger or
1 tsp fresh ginger, minced
3 T soy sauce

In a wok or large frying pan, stir-fry pork and shrimp in 1 tablespoon oil until pork is no longer pink. Remove and set aside. Heat remaining tablespoon oil and add scallions, cabbage, carrots and seasonings. Continue to stir-fry until cabbage wilts. Add bean sprouts and pork/shrimp mixture. Remove from heat and cool.

EGG ROLLS:

1 lb egg roll wrappers (16)

1 egg, beaten with 1 tsp water

Place square egg roll wrapper with a corner pointing toward you. Put ¼ to ⅓ cup cooled filling on wrapper slightly below center. Brush edges with beaten egg. Fold corner nearest to you up and over filling, jellyroll fashion. Then fold left corner over, then fold over the right corner. Roll towards top corner to form a cylinder. Brush with egg mixture. Cover with a damp towel until ready to use. Deep-fry in wok or electric skillet at 375° until golden. Drain and serve with duck sauce. These can also be made into cocktail-size egg rolls by using wonton wrappers and following the same procedure.

Yield: approximately 16 full-size egg rolls or 64 cocktail-size egg rolls

Hint: *These are a favorite with my children and in my Chinese cooking classes! The filling can be made several hours or a day ahead. Once filled, the egg rolls may be frozen. To serve after having been frozen, remove from freezer and heat at 350° for 15 to 20 minutes or until hot.*

4

BAKED WONTONS

12 wonton wrappers
Nonstick spray coating or
2 tsp margarine, melted

2 T Parmesan cheese, grated
¼ to ½ tsp basil

Spray a 10½"x15½" cookie sheet with nonstick spray coating. Cut wonton wrappers in half diagonally and place on a cookie sheet. Spray wrappers with nonstick spray or brush with melted margarine. Sprinkle with Parmesan cheese and basil. Bake at 400° for 4 to 5 minutes or until crisp.

Yield: 24 baked wontons

Hint: Usually when one thinks of wontons, words such as fried, fattening and high in fat come to mind. However, these wonton crisps are low in fat and calories and even taste good, too! Sesame seeds, minced garlic or any combination of herbs may be used instead of, or in addition to, Parmesan cheese.

CRAB RANGOONS

1 lb wonton wrappers or 1 lb egg
roll wrappers, cut in quarters
8 oz cream cheese, softened
8 oz crabmeat or surimi
(imitation crab)

¼ to ½ tsp cayenne pepper,
or crushed dried red pepper
flakes, to taste
2 to 3 T water
Oil for frying

Combine all ingredients except wonton wrappers. Place ½ to 1 teaspoon crab mixture in a corner of the wonton and roll up on the diagonal. Moisten tips of wonton wrappers with water to seal. Place seam side down in 1½ to 2 inches hot oil and fry until golden on one side. Turn over and fry until second side is golden. Remove from oil and drain on paper towels.

Yield: approximately 64 rangoons

Hint: Serve with duck sauce or hot mustard. These may be frozen. To reheat, place frozen rangoons in a 350° oven and bake until hot, about 10 minutes. You can substitute a 6½ ounce can of tuna for the crab.

BAKED BRIE CHEESE

8 oz Brie cheese, round or wedge
2 T honey mustard

2 to 3 T sliced almonds

Place Brie cheese in a pie plate or other oven proof dish. Spread with honey mustard. Then sprinkle with sliced almonds. Bake at 350° for 10 to 12 minutes, depending on size of cheese, or until cheese is soft and just begins to run. Serve with chunks of fresh crusty bread and slices of apples and pears.

Hint: You may use a larger piece of Brie and adjust other ingredients accordingly. Brown sugar may be substituted for the honey mustard. The Brie may be baked in the microwave on medium for 2 to 3 minutes, or until the cheese melts.

CRAB NACHOS

32 nacho chips
8 oz crabmeat or surimi
(imitation crab)

3 to 4 T salsa
1½ C Monterey Jack
cheese, shredded

Place nacho chips on a greased baking sheet. Top each with a small mound of crab. Drizzle about ¼ teaspoon salsa over crab and cover with cheese. Bake at 400° for about 5 minutes, or just until cheese is melted. The nachos may be refrigerated overnight or frozen.

Yield: 32 crab nachos

Hint: These are elegant and yet easy to prepare. If freezing, do not defrost before baking, but bake for 8 to 10 minutes or until heated through.

6

POTATO NACHOS

1 large baking potato, cut
into ¼" slices
Salt, to taste
½ C taco sauce

2 T pimento, chopped
2 T pitted black olives,
sliced (optional)
⅓ C Cheddar cheese, shredded

Place potato slices on a microwave-safe plate in a single layer. Sprinkle with salt, if desired. Brush with taco sauce. Cover with plastic wrap, turning back one corner to vent. Microwave on high 4 to 5 minutes, turning once. Top with pimentos, olives and cheese. Cover and microwave on high 30 to 40 seconds or until cheese is melted. Serve with remaining taco sauce.

Hint: This is a quick, healthy snack that is good for almost any time. Using potatoes, instead of nacho chips, cuts down on fat, calories and salt. It is also high in fiber and very filling.

MINI-PEPPERONI CHEESE ROLLS

1 pkg Pillsbury Crescent Rolls
4 oz pepperoni, sliced

4 oz Cheddar cheese, shredded
1 egg, beaten with 1 tsp water

Open Crescent Roll package. Press 2 triangles (a quarter of the dough) together and roll out slightly with rolling pin into an oblong shape. Spread a quarter of pepperoni slices on dough. Cover with a quarter of the cheese. Roll up, jellyroll fashion, and pinch ends to seal. Place seam side down on a greased cookie sheet. Brush with egg mixture. Bake at 375° for 10 to 12 minutes, or until golden. Allow to cool for about 2 to 3 minutes before slicing. Serve hot.

Yield: 32 pieces

Hint: Slice each roll into about 8 pieces to serve as hors d'oeuvres. If you want to serve these as sandwiches, do not cut them and you will have 4 sandwiches. These pepperoni rolls make a hit with "kids" of all ages.

RIED ARTICHOKES

14 oz can artichoke hearts (packed in water), drained
¼ C flour
½ to ¾ C Parmesan cheese, freshly grated

1 egg, beaten with 1 T water
⅛ tsp garlic powder
Salt and pepper, to taste
¼ C canola or olive oil

Mix flour with garlic powder, salt and pepper. Beat egg, water and Parmesan cheese together. Cut artichoke hearts in half and squeeze gently to remove excess liquid. Roll each artichoke half in seasoned flour and then dip into egg mixture. Fry in oil until golden on all sides. Drain on paper towels.

Yield: 12 to 16 artichoke halves. (Each can contains 6 to 8 artichokes.)

Hint: These may be frozen. To heat at a later date, partially defrost and heat at 350° for about 10 minutes, or until hot. Zucchini, broccoli and mushrooms may be fried using the same batter.

ERIYAKI SIRLOIN ROLL-UPS

1½ lbs stir-fry beef or boneless sirloin steak, cut into ¾" slices
1 tsp ginger
½ C soy sauce

¼ C canola oil
1 clove garlic, minced
2 T brown sugar
20 oz can pineapple chunks, drained (save juice)

Combine ginger, soy sauce, oil, garlic, brown sugar and juice from pineapple. Add slices of beef and mix well. Marinate several hours or overnight. Cut pineapple chunks in half. Remove steak from marinade and roll each piece around a halved pineapple chunk. Secure with toothpick. Broil 3 to 4 inches from heat for 2 minutes on each side.

WISS SANDWICH PUFFS

32 slices party rye bread, toasted
½ C mayonnaise
¼ C onion, finely chopped

2 T parsley, finely chopped
⅓ lb Swiss cheese, sliced

Combine mayonnaise, onion and parsley. Spread on rye bread. Top each with a piece of Swiss cheese. Broil 2 to 3 minutes, or until cheese is bubbly.

Hint: If you use a food processor to make the mayonnaise topping this recipe is a cinch.

Mushroom Turnovers

DOUGH:

8 oz cream cheese, softened

½ C butter or margarine

1½ C flour

Combine cream cheese, butter and flour in a large bowl. Beat well until soft dough forms. Wrap in plastic wrap and refrigerate for at least one hour, or overnight.

FILLING:

½ lb mushrooms, minced

3 T butter or margarine

1 large onion, minced

½ tsp salt

¼ tsp thyme

2 T flour

¼ C sour cream

1 egg, beaten with 1 tsp water

Sauté mushrooms and onions in butter or margarine for about 5 minutes, or until tender. Stir in salt, thyme and flour until blended. Add sour cream and mix well. Cool. Roll out half the dough on a floured board. Cut out 3-inch circles of dough with a cookie cutter or glass. Brush edges of circles with egg wash made of egg and water beaten together. Place 1 teaspoon filling on half of circle. Fold other half over filling to meet other edges. Press edges together with tines of a fork to form a turnover. Pierce top of turnover to act as steam vents. Place on greased cookie sheet. Brush turnovers with egg mixture. Repeat with other half of dough. Bake at 450° for 12 to 15 minutes, or until golden brown.

Hint: After turnovers are brushed with egg wash, they may be frozen before being baked. They may then be removed from freezer, placed on cookie sheets and baked as directed.

HOT CLAM OR CRAB DIP

8 oz fresh minced clams, or crab meat or imitation crab (surimi)	2 tsp Worcestershire sauce
8 oz cream cheese	2 T onion, chopped
1 T milk	2 T slivered almonds, toasted

Combine cream cheese, milk and Worcestershire sauce. Add minced clams or flaked crab meat to cream cheese mixture. Add onion. Place in a greased shallow casserole dish or pie plate and top with almonds. Bake at 350° for 15 minutes.

Microwave: Heat on medium 4 to 8 minutes until smooth, stirring every 2 minutes.

Hint: The fresh clams are the key ingredient in this recipe. They are far superior to canned clams. To toast almonds, bake at 350° for 3 to 5 minutes.

CHEESE PENNIES

½ lb sharp Cheddar cheese, shredded	½ tsp salt, or to taste
¼ lb butter or margarine, softened	1½ C flour, sifted
	Dash cayenne pepper

Cream the cheese and butter or margarine thoroughly. Blend in flour, salt and cayenne and work into a smooth dough. Form dough into rolls about 1 inch in diameter and wrap in wax paper. Refrigerate for at least 2 hours or up to 2 days. Slice rolls into wafers about ⅓-inch thick. Arange on ungreased cookie sheet. Bake at 400° for 12 to 15 minutes, or until golden.

Yield: 2 dozen

Hint: These may be made in advance and kept in a tin for a few days before serving.

10

NISHES

DOUGH:

1 pkg dry yeast
¼ C lukewarm water
½ lb butter or margarine
2 C flour

1 T sugar
3 egg yolks
Few grains salt
1 egg yolk, to brush on knishes

Dissolve yeast in lukewarm water (105 to 115°). Set aside. In large mixing bowl, cut butter or margarine into dry ingredients. Add dissolved yeast and 3 egg yolks. Combine and knead by hand until smooth. Wrap ball of dough in waxed paper and refrigerate at least 2 hours, preferably overnight. Divide dough into 5 parts. Roll out dough into a rectangle on a floured pastry board or counter. Place filling along the edge of the dough that is nearest to you and roll up jellyroll fashion. Cut into 1-inch slices and place on an ungreased cookie sheet. Cover with a towel and let rise for 30 minutes to 1 hour. Brush top of knishes with a beaten egg yolk. Bake at 400° for 15 to 20 minutes, or until golden.

Yield: 5 to 8 dozen

Hint: To freeze, "flash freeze" on a cookie sheet. When firm enough to pull off sheet, place knishes in foil pans and wrap in plastic bags or wrap in freezer bags. To reheat, place knishes in a 400° oven for 15 to 18 minutes or until hot. Cover top with foil so they do not overbrown.

FILLING VARIATIONS:

POTATO

2 large onions, diced
¼ C chicken fat or margarine
2 C mashed potatoes

1 egg
1 tsp salt
¼ tsp pepper

Brown the onions in the chicken fat or margarine. Add potatoes, egg, salt and pepper. Mix until smooth.

MEAT

½ C onions, minced
2 T chicken fat or margarine
1½ C cooked leftover beef, or cooked hamburg

1 egg
1 tsp salt
¼ tsp pepper

Lightly brown onions in chicken fat or margarine. Add meat, egg, salt and pepper. Mix until smooth.

Hint: This was one of my "signature recipes" for my first cooking classes. I still use it when I have large parties because it yields a large amount, freezes well and always disappears quickly because people adore them! Don't be discouraged by the length of the recipe; it is not complicated and is fun to make! These will keep in the freezer for up to 2 months; so if you're planning a party they can be made well in advance.

11

MINI-REUBEN SANDWICHES

2 loaves cocktail rye bread
¾ lb Swiss cheese, thinly sliced
1½ lbs corned beef
16 to 24 oz sauerkraut, well drained

6 to 8 oz Thousand Island
or Russian salad dressing
Butter or margarine

Spread several pieces of bread on counter at a time. Spread one side of each sandwich with salad dressing. Top with cheese, sauerkraut and corned beef. Place other half of sandwich on top. Place in frying pan or on grill and cook in butter or margarine until cheese melts and sandwich is crispy. Instead of grilling these, they may be baked at 400° for 5 to 7 minutes, or until sandwiches are hot and the cheese melted.

Yield: 42 to 44 mini sandwiches

MINI-RACHEL SANDWICHES

Make these the same way as the Reubens except substitute turkey breast for corned beef. To make the Rachels lower in cholesterol, fat and sodium, substitute low fat Swiss cheese, low salt turkey breast and low calorie or fat free Thousand Island or Russian salad dressing.

Hint: The sauerkraut that is packed in jars or cryovac, usually kosher or deli style, is much tastier to use in this recipe than a canned sauerkraut. Use cole slaw as an alternative to sauerkraut.

ZIPPY COCKTAIL FRANKS

¾ C prepared mustard
10 oz jar currant jelly

2 lbs cocktail franks

Whisk mustard and jelly together over low heat until melted and smooth. Add franks which have been boiled very briefly. When ready to serve, transfer to a chafing dish.

Hint: This is an OBG, oldies but goodies, recipe. The reason this recipe has been around so long is because it is so good and easy! If you can't find cocktail franks, cut up regular-size frankfurts into bite-size pieces.

CAPE COD HERRING AND CRANBERRY DIP

1 lb jar herring fillet "tidbits
in wine sauce" sliced
16 oz can whole cranberry sauce

1 large red onion, sliced
1 pt sour cream

Drain herring. Discard white onions from herring jar. Combine cranberries and sour cream. Fold in herring and red onion. Marinate 24 hours before serving.

Hint: This cranberry herring dip, which is a beautiful pink color, is delicious for brunch or a cocktail party. It is very easy to prepare and can be made 2 to 3 days in advance. An attractive way to serve it is to place the dip in a round loaf of pumpernickel bread that has been hollowed out. To hollow the bread, cut a slice off the top and use a grapefruit knife to make a circular cut all around the inside edge of the bread. Then cut out the filling from the loaf and cut it into chunks. Place these chunks around the base of the bread to serve as dippers. Serve with additional party rye.

CHUTNEY CHEESE DIP

1 lb cream cheese, softened
9 oz jar mango chutney

1 large pineapple
Sesame sticks

Chop the chutney by hand or in a food processor, using steel blade. Add the cheese and mix well. This should be done a day or two before serving so that the flavors will be well blended. To serve, twist off the stem of the pineapple and set aside. Cut pineapple in half lengthwise. Use a grapefruit knife to scoop out flesh of 1 pineapple half. Cut flesh into cubes. Cut up remaining half of pineapple into cubes. Turn one empty half upside down to drain and dry with paper towels. When pineapple shell is dry, just before serving, fill with cream cheese chutney dip. Use pineapple cubes and sesame sticks as dippers.

Hint: Twisting off the stem of the pineapple makes it easier to cut. Also, you can stand up the stem as a decoration on the platter on which you are serving the dip. Chutney is in the supermarket near pickles and olives.

13

COTTAGE CHEESE HERB DIP

1 lb cottage cheese
4 T Parmesan cheese, grated
2 T mayonnaise
1 T onion, minced
1 T parsley, minced

1 tsp Worcestershire sauce
1 tsp garlic powder or
    fresh garlic, to taste
1 tsp oregano

Place all ingredients in a blender or food processor and process until smooth. Serve with fresh vegetables and/or crackers or bread sticks.

Hint: *If nonfat cottage cheese and cholesterol free mayonnaise are used, this dip will be very low in cholesterol and fat.*

CREAMY SALSA DIP

2 C plain yogurt

1½ C salsa

Drain yogurt in a strainer lined with cheese cloth or in the top of a drip coffee pot filter lined with a paper filter and set over a bowl. Refrigerate for 4 to 8 hours, or overnight, until the water or whey has drained off and a thicker mass called yogurt cheese remains. Then add salsa and mix well. Serve with nacho chips or crudites.

Hint: *Use nonfat plain yogurt if you want a completely fat free dip. The longer you drain yogurt, the firmer it will get. Add herbs or spices for a savory dip or spread. Add jam, honey, grated orange or lemon rind or coconut to use as a fruit dip or spread.*

14

CURRIED SALMON OR TUNA SALAD ON CUCUMBER SLICES

6½ or 7 oz can salmon or tuna
¼ C currants
¼ C pecans, toasted and chopped
¼ C mayonnaise
2 cucumbers, unpeeled and sliced ¼" thick

1 T red wine vinegar
2 T chutney, chopped
Curry powder, to taste
¼ C parsley, minced
Wedges of red and green pepper

Drain the salmon or tuna well and put it in a mixing bowl or bowl of a food processor. Add the remaining ingredients and mix well. Refrigerate until ready to use. With a melon baller or tip of a teaspoon, place a small scoop of the mixture on each cucumber slice or fill pepper wedges with mixture. This spread is also delicious on party rye bread, crackers, or on a roll or croissant as a sandwich.

Hint: To toast pecans, bake at 350° for 3 to 4 minutes. Chutney is usually near the pickles and olives in the supermarket. The steel bade of a food processor makes it easy to mince the parsley and chop the pecans and the chutney. Just add the remaining ingredients. If low fat or cholesterol free mayonnaise is used, this is a very healthy spread. Also, to decorate the cucumber, run a lemon stripper or the tines of a fork down the length of the cucumber before slicing it.

EASY SALMON SPREAD

3 oz pkg cream cheese, softened to room temperature
6½ to 7 oz can salmon, drained and flaked

1 T scallions, minced
1 tsp oregano
¼ tsp Tobasco sauce
Dash liquid smoke

Combine all ingredients; mix well. Chill in a small crock, about 1 cup capacity. Serve with fresh vegetables or crackers.

Hint: This is quick and easy to make and may be prepared at least a day in advance.

16

𝒫INE CONE CHEESE SPREAD

8 oz cold pack Cheddar cheese
4 oz cream cheese
1 T butter
Horseradish

Worcestershire sauce
Dry sherry
1 C pecan halves

With electric mixer, cream together first three ingredients until well blended. Add horseradish, Worcestershire sauce and sherry to taste. Cover and chill for several hours or even a few days. Remove from refrigerator and shape on a serving platter to resemble a pine cone. Insert rounded edges of pecans into cheese in rows. Garnish with sprigs of fresh parsley at wide end. Serve with crackers.

Hint: This is very pretty to serve in the fall and at the holiday season. It's even a nice spread served from a crock, omitting the pecans.

ℋOLIDAY CHEESE BALL

¾ lb cream cheese
¼ lb butter
3 to 4 oz pimento (often called roasted peppers), chopped

2 to 3 oz black olives, chopped
Green of 2 scallions, chopped
1 tsp sweet relish
Walnuts or pecans, chopped

Melt butter and blend with softened cream cheese. Add remaining ingredients and mix thoroughly. Shape into a ball and roll in chopped nuts. Serve with crackers.

Hint: This cheese ball is always a hit, but is especially nice to serve during the holidays because when you spread it on a cracker you see the red and green colors of the vegetables. Pimento is usually found in 4-ounce jars near the pickles and relishes in the supermarket.

HONEY MUSTARD DIP

1 C mayonnaise
1 C low fat cottage cheese
¼ C honey
¼ C Dijon mustard

¼ C cider vinegar
2 T fresh parsley, chopped
1 small onion, finely chopped

Mix cottage cheese, parsley and onion in a blender or food processor, using the steel blade, until quite smooth. Add remaining ingredients and mix well. Chill overnight or for at least a few hours. Serve with crudities (fresh vegetables) or crackers.

Hint: If you use cholesterol free mayonnaise and low fat cottage cheese, this dip is low in cholesterol. If cottage cheese is omitted, you may use as a salad dressing.

MEXICAN DIP

2 16 oz cans or 3 11½ oz
jars refried beans
2 to 3 avocados, peeled and mashed
1 pt sour cream
1 pkg taco seasoning mix
1 C black olives, sliced

1 bunch scallions, sliced
2 to 3 tomatoes, chopped
6 to 8 oz Cheddar or Monterey
Jack cheese, shredded
Nacho chips

Mash refried beans and spread on a large serving platter leaving a border around the edge. Peel and mash avocados and spread over beans, leaving a 1-inch border of beans showing around edge. Combine sour cream and taco seasoning mix and spread on top as next layer, again leaving a 1-inch border around edge. Continue by layering remaining ingredients in the order listed, ending with cheese on top. Place nacho chips around edge of platter to scoop up layered dip. Serve extra nacho chips in a basket.

Hint: You can use this dip as a salad or place it in a taco shell as an entree. Also, if mashing avocado in advance, drizzle with fresh lemon juice to prevent it from discoloring.

NIPPY FISH DIP

1 lb gefilte fish, drained and mashed
¼ C celery, finely chopped
1 tsp onion, grated

¼ C mayonnaise
¼ C butter or margarine, softened
2 T horseradish

Mash gefilte fish and add remaining ingredients. Blend well by hand or in food processor, using steel blade. Serve with matzoh, crackers or crudities.

Hint: *Gefilte fish is available in the kosher section of most supermarkets. It is sold in both jars and cans.*

EGGPLANT DIP

1 medium eggplant, cubed with skin
1 medium onion, chopped
4 oz can mushrooms, drained
½ C olive oil
6 oz can tomato paste
½ C water

2 T wine vinegar
1½ tsp sugar
½ tsp salt
½ tsp oregano
⅛ tsp pepper

Saute eggplant, onion and mushrooms in oil for 10 minutes in a covered frying pan. Put mixture in food processor or blender and process or blend just until smooth. Put mixture back in pan and add remaining ingredients. Cook over low heat for 30 minutes, mixing occasionally. Serve warm or at room temperature in fresh hollowed-out rye or pumpernickel bread.

Hint: *This dip is low in cholesterol and a nice change from the usual cheese dips.*

ZIPPY DIP

1 C low fat or nonfat cottage cheese   1 to 2 T horseradish sauce
2 T sweet red pepper relish

Mix all ingredients together in food processor, using steel blade, until desired consistency is reached. Serve with crackers or vegetables.

Hint: When you taste this dip you'll realize how it got its name! Adjust the amounts of horseradish and relish to suit your taste. This really is a low fat dip, especially if you use nonfat cottage cheese. If you are really watching your cholesterol, you may want to make your own Horseradish Sauce because most commercial ones contain egg yolk. To make your own horseradish sauce: mix 1 tablespoon cholesterol free or fat free mayonnaise with 1 teaspoon horseradish. This dip may be made several days in advance and looks pretty when served in a hollowed-out green, red or yellow pepper that has been zigzag cut. You can make zigzag cuts in peppers, oranges or melons with a sharp paring knife or a gadget called a V-cut or decorating knife. I have served this dip at many demonstrations and parties and everyone, even people who usually don't like cottage cheese, loved it!

SMOKED OYSTER ROLL

8 oz pkg cream cheese
2 T mayonnaise
½ tsp garlic, minced
Dash Worcestershire sauce
Salt and pepper, to taste

3½ oz can smoked oysters, chopped
½ C pecans, toasted and coarsely chopped

Soften cream cheese and mix with everything but oysters and pecans. Spread pecans on wax paper into a rectangle about 6"x8". Spread cream cheese mixture on top of pecans. Refrigerate for at least 1 hour. Remove from refrigerator and spread oysters on top of cream cheese. Use wax paper to roll up this layered rectangle, jellyroll fashion, into a log. Remove wax paper. Garnish with parsley and serve with plain crackers.

Hint: This roll is nice to serve when you are looking for something different to serve with the usual crackers and cheese. To toast pecans, bake at 350° for 3 to 5 minutes, watching carefully not to burn them.

BROCCOLI AND CAULIFLOWER BUSH

3 to 4 lbs broccoli
3 to 4 lbs cauliflower (2 medium heads)

Cut the stalks off the broccoli and trim it into serving-size flowerets. Remove the core from the cauliflowers and cut into serving-size flowerets. Boil a large pot of salted water. Cook the cauliflower until crisp-tender, about 3 to 4 minutes. Remove it with a slotted spoon and place it in a bowl of cold water to stop the cooking. Add the broccoli to the boiling water and cook until crisp-tender, 2 to 3 minutes, being careful not to overcook. Place the broccoli in a bowl of cold water. Drain the vegetables well and blot on paper towels.

Choose a 2 to 3-quart deep, round bowl and, beginning in the center, alternate circles of the vegetables, floweret side down, covering the bottom and the sides of the bowl. Continue layering rows, fitting the vegetables as close together as possible and making sure the center of the bowl is well packed with flowerets so that the vegetables are actually sticking up over the top of the bowl. Place a plate over the vegetables and weigh down with books, cans, an iron or any other heavy object. Refrigerate for at least 8 hours or overnight. Before serving, remove weights and invert the bowl over the sink, holding the plate and pouring off any excess liquid. Invert onto a platter. Serve with a cold dip.

Hint: This makes a beautiful, edible centerpiece, especially during the holiday season. Surround the platter with hollowed-out red peppers filled with dip, as well as cut-up red and green vegetables, such as cherry tomatoes, radishes, red peppers, celery, cucumbers and green peppers. Although this is a lengthy recipe, it is not difficult to make and it will be worth the effort when you see how people compliment you. The "bush" may be made up to 2 days in advance, refrigerated and then unmolded an hour or two before serving.

PICKLED MUSHROOMS

⅓ C wine vinegar   1 tsp brown sugar
⅓ C canola or olive oil   1 tsp mustard (prepared)
1 T parsley, chopped   1 lb mushrooms

Boil everything except mushrooms. Add mushrooms. Simmer 5 minutes, stirring continuously. Place in jars and refrigerate.

Hint: These mushrooms will keep for 2 weeks in the refrigerator. They make lovely gifts, especially if you use decorative jars. Be sure to tell the recipient that these must be refrigerated.

SALMON MOUSSE

15 to 16 oz can salmon, drained
and finely flaked
1 C onion, finely chopped
1 C celery, finely chopped
Salt and pepper, to taste
10¾ oz can tomato soup

8 oz cream cheese
1 C mayonnaise
2 dashes Tobasco sauce
1 T Worcestershire sauce
2 T unflavored gelatin
¼ C cold water

Mix salmon, onion and celery together. Over low heat, whisk soup and cream cheese together until smooth. Remove from heat and whisk in mayonnaise, Tobasco and Worcestershire. Set aside. Blend gelatin and water together until gelatin dissolves. Add this to mayonnaise mixture. Fold in salmon. Blend well. Season with salt and pepper, if necessary. Pour into a greased 5½ cup mold. Chill for several hours or overnight.

Hint: This looks especially beautiful in a fish-shaped mold, garnished with olives, pimento and thinly sliced cucumbers. If you don't have a fish mold, any shape will do. This makes a wonderful appetizer with crackers or party rye. It also may be used as an entree for brunch or a light luncheon. It is best made 1 to 2 days ahead.

SHRIMP WRAPPED IN PEA PODS

1 lb shrimp (28 to 30), peeled
and deveined

15 pea pods

DRESSING:

½ C olive oil
3 T fresh lemon juice
3 T Dijon mustard

2 cloves garlic, finely minced
Dash sugar
Salt and pepper, to taste

Peel and devein shrimp. Place them in a large pot of boiling water and cook for 2 to 3 minutes, or until just done (shrimp will begin curling up and turning pink). Immerse shrimp in ice cold water to cool. Drain well. Shake dressing ingredients in a covered jar and pour over shrimp. Shrimp may be marinated in this dressing for a day in advance of serving. A few hours before serving, destring pea pods and blanch in boiling water for 30 seconds. Immediately immerse in ice cold water. Drain well. With a sharp knife split the pea pods in half lengthwise so you have 30 separate halves. Chill. Just before serving, drain shrimp and wrap each one with a pea pod half and fasten with a toothpick.

Hint: If you want to save time, buy cooked and cleaned shrimp. You may make the dressing several days in advance.

21

HRIMP STUFFED CHERRY TOMATOES

1 lb cherry tomatoes	2 tsp horseradish
1 lb shrimp, peeled, cooked and chopped	¼ C chili sauce
	1 C celery, finely chopped
¼ C sour cream	¼ tsp salt, or to taste

Wash and drain tomatoes. Cut a thin slice off the top of each tomato and, using a melon baller, scoop out the pulp. Turn tomatoes upside down and drain. Combine remaining ingredients, stuff into tomato shells and refrigerate.

Hint: The tomatoes may be stuffed up to 2 hours before serving. The shrimp mixture is also delicious served with crackers, party rye bread or vegetables. Cherry tomatoes may also be filled with herb cheese, hummus or Tabbouli (pg. 51).

OT BERRY CIDER

1 qt apple cider	2 cinnamon sticks
1 qt cranberry juice	½ tsp whole cloves
2 T brown sugar	

Pour cider and juice into a large saucepan. Add brown sugar. Place cinnamon sticks and cloves in a piece of cheesecloth and tie together. Add to saucepan. Bring mixture to a boil and then reduce to simmer for 15 minutes. Remove cheesecloth. Serve hot.

Hint: This is delicious on a cold fall or winter day, especially after apple picking or sledding. You can pour it into a thermos and bring it to a tailgate picnic.

FESTIVE PUNCH

ICE MOLD:

10 oz frozen raspberries, defrosted
2 limes, thinly sliced

Pineapple juice or water

Make ice mold several days in advance by combining raspberries, lime slices and enough pineapple juice or water to fill a 4-cup mold or any size you choose. Freeze.

PUNCH:

46 oz pineapple juice
1 liter ginger ale
1 liter raspberry soda

1 qt raspberry sherbert
1 lime, sliced
½ pt raspberries

To serve punch, place ice mold and sherbert in punch bowl. Pour pineapple juice and both sodas on top. Garnish with additional raspberries and lime slices, if desired.

Hint: This is the easiest and most delicious punch for groups of any age and for any occasion. It is refreshing and easy to keep refilling during a party. Add liquor if you like, but it is delicious as is.

MULLED CRAN-APRICOT TEA

2 C (½ lb) cranberries
3 sticks cinnamon
1 T orange rind, grated
6 oz can frozen orange juice
1 qt apricot nectar

4 cloves
3 6 oz cans water
½ C sugar, or less, to taste
8 small cinnamon sticks or
8 orange slices (for garnish)

In a 2 to 3-quart saucepan, combine the cranberries, apricot nectar, cinnamon, cloves and orange rind. Over moderately high heat, bring to a boil, stirring occasionally. Boil until the cranberries pop. Strain the liquid into a large bowl, discarding the spices and berries. Add the frozen juice, water and sugar. Stir until the sugar is dissolved. Refrigerate the "tea" until serving time and cover the bowl with plastic wrap or transfer it to bottles. Just before serving, pour the "tea" into a large nonaluminum pot or kettle and, over moderately high heat, bring it to just below the boiling point. Pour into heated mugs and garnish with sticks of cinnamon or orange slices.

Hint: This is a lovely beverage to serve around the holiday season. It is especially nice at a brunch, tea or late afternoon open house.

Soups

CREAM OF BROCCOLI, CAULIFLOWER OR ZUCCHINI SOUP

8 C broth, chicken or beef (or half of each)
4 C broccoli, cauliflower or zucchini (or combination), roughly chopped
1 medium onion, chopped
1 C medium cream, milk or yogurt

2 to 4 T dry sherry or marsala
Salt and pepper, to taste
½ C sour cream or yogurt, for garnish
1 to 2 T chives, chopped

Cook the vegetables and onions in broth until tender, about 20 minutes. Puree in a food processor or blender. Return to the stove and add the sherry or marsala. Add the cream, milk or yogurt and mix well. Season with salt and pepper, to taste. Combine the sour cream or yogurt with the chives and use as a garnish, if desired. Serve either hot or cold.

Hint: This is one of the easiest and healthiest soups to make. If you use milk or yogurt, it is almost fat and calorie free. You can use your own broth or use canned or good quality bouillon cubes. This soup is equally delicious served hot or cold. It freezes well; however, it is better to freeze it before adding the cream or yogurt.

PLIT PEA SOUP

8 C chicken or vegetable broth
2 C split peas, rinsed
2 bay leaves
2 cloves garlic, minced
1 stalk celery, chopped
2 carrots, chopped
1 onion, minced

1 potato, peeled and cubed
2 T fresh parsley, minced
¼ tsp thyme
½ tsp marjoram
1½ tsp soy sauce
Black pepper, to taste

Bring the broth to a boil. Add the split peas and bay leaves. Cover and simmer for 30 minutes. Add the vegetables, herbs and seasonings to the soup. Simmer until the vegetables are soft, about 30 to 35 minutes. Remove the bay leaves before serving.

Hint: This is a very healthy and hearty soup. Split peas are high in protein and low in fat. When combined with a grain, such as bread, they can serve as a "complete meal". This soup is very inexpensive and freezes beautifully. In fact, I usually make a double batch and freeze the leftover in freezer bags or plastic containers.

INESTRONE SOUP

3 medium onions, diced
2 carrots, sliced
2 stalks celery, sliced
4 medium potatoes, peeled and cubed
2 medium zucchini, cubed
2 C green cabbage, shredded
½ lb green beans, halved
2 cloves garlic, minced
¼ C olive oil
8 C water

28 oz can tomatoes or 2 lbs
   ripe fresh tomatoes
3 beef bouillon cubes or 3 C
   beef broth
1 tsp oregano
½ tsp basil
2 C spaghetti, broken
   into 1" pieces
Parmesan cheese or pesto
   sauce (for garnish)

Saute the onion and garlic in olive oil in a large pot until golden. Add the remaining ingredients except for spaghetti. Cover and simmer for 2 to 2½ hours. Add the spaghetti and cook 10 minutes more. If desired, garnish with Parmesan cheese and/or Pesto Sauce (pg.133).

Hint: This tastes even more delicious if you add some soup bones to the pot instead of, or in addition to, the bouillon. This soup freezes well so you may like to make a double batch and freeze half of it.

APPLE AND BUTTERNUT SQUASH BISQUE

2 Granny Smith apples, peeled, seeded and coarsely chopped
1 small (1 lb) butternut squash, unpeeled, seeded and cut in half
1 medium onion, coarsely chopped
Pinch rosemary
Pinch thyme

1 qt chicken broth
2 slices white bread, trimmed and cubed
½ tsp salt, or to taste
¼ tsp pepper
½ C light or medium cream

Combine everything except cream in a large saucepan. Bring to a boil and simmer uncovered for 45 minutes, or until vegetables are soft. Scoop out the squash pulp and discard the skin. Return the squash pulp to the pan. Puree the entire mixture in a food processor or blender. Return the puree to the saucepan. Add the cream and then heat, but do not boil.

Hint: If desired, pre-cook the squash in the microwave. Wash the squash and prick it all over with the tines of a fork. Cook on high for 10 minutes. Cool and cut open. Remove the seeds. Scoop out the flesh and put it in the saucepan with all the other ingredients. Reduce simmering time to 35 minutes. This soup is perfect for a tailgate picnic on a brisk fall day. It can easily be kept hot in a thermos and served in mugs. Bread sticks or croutons are a good accompaniment.

QUICK CORN CHOWDER

16 oz can cream style corn
16 oz milk
1 large potato, diced
1 green pepper, diced

1 medium onion, diced
1 T butter or margarine
Salt and pepper, to taste

Boil diced potato until almost tender and set aside. Melt butter or margarine in a 2-quart saucepan. Add onion and pepper and saute until tender. Add corn, milk, potato, salt and pepper. Stir and bring to a boil. Immediately reduce to a simmer and cook for 15 to 20 minutes or until potato is tender. Adjust seasoning.

Hint: Since I've gotten this recipe, I always keep a can of creamed corn handy. The other ingredients are usually staples in my house so I use this as an emergency dish on a cold fall or winter evening. It's a real comfort food that everyone enjoys.

GGPLANT POTAGE

1½ C onion, diced
1½ C celery, diced
1 large eggplant, diced
1½ C potatoes, diced
3 T butter or margarine, melted
½ tsp curry powder
2 tsp Worcestershire sauce

½ tsp basil
1 tsp thyme
1 tsp salt, or to taste
⅛ tsp pepper
4 C chicken broth
2 C light or medium cream

Saute onion, celery, eggplant and potatoes in melted butter or margarine. Add seasonings and cook, uncovered, over medium heat until potatoes are tender. Stir often. Stir in chicken broth and cook until soup begins to thicken, about 45 minutes. Mash vegetables with a potato masher if chunky soup is desired. If smooth soup is desired, place contents in blender or processor and blend until smooth. Then add cream. Simmer a few minutes until heated through.

Hint: This soup has a robust flavor and an interesting texture.

ROUND BEEF AND BARLEY SOUP

1 T canola or olive oil
1 C onion, chopped
1 lb lean ground beef
5 C beef broth
1 C water
½ C celery, sliced
1 C carrot, diced
1½ C tomatoes, peeled and chopped

¼ C barley
1 T tomato paste
1 bay leaf
¼ tsp black pepper
½ tsp basil
Parmesan or Romano cheese, grated (for garnish)

Heat oil in a large pot. Add the onion and saute until soft. Add beef and cook until it loses its red color. Then add the remaining ingredients. Boil and reduce to a simmer. Cover and simmer for 40 to 45 minutes, or until barley is tender. Garnish with fresh grated cheese just before serving.

Hint: This soup is a complete meal. If you like, you can substitute ground chicken or turkey for the ground beef. Serve with fresh bread and a salad. Leftovers taste good for a few days.

FISH AND CORN CHOWDER

2 medium onions, chopped
2 T butter or margarine
4 C potato, peeled and diced
1 lb "fish pieces" or any firm white
fish such as scrod, haddock,
hake, etc.

12 oz can evaporated milk
16 oz can cream style corn
1 tsp salt, or to taste
¼ tsp pepper, or to taste
1 C water

Saute onions in butter or margarine until soft. Add potatoes and water and cover. Simmer for about 15 minutes, or until potatoes are almost tender. Add fish and cook for about 5 to 7 minutes. Then add remaining ingredients and heat just until boiling.

Hint: By using "fish pieces" or "chowder fish", or whatever firm white fish is on special, you can make a delicious and economical meal. This is especially welcome on a cold fall or winter evening. Serve with some crusty bread and a green salad.

TURKEY SOUP

Cooked turkey carcass, with most
of meat removed
4 stalks celery, sliced
3 onions, sliced

3 carrots, sliced
2 to 3 T salt, or to taste
¼ tsp pepper, or to taste
Water

Place all the ingredients in a large saucepan and add enough water to cover. Bring to a boil; reduce heat and simmer, uncovered, for 2 hours or until the liquid is reduced by half. Strain and refrigerate. When it is cold, remove any congealed fat from the top.

Hint: This is a good way to recycle your turkey leftovers. We recycle everything else these days so why not recycle this? The resulting broth may be used in other soup recipes, or as a base for sauces. If you don't need the broth within a few days, freeze it.

29

ONTON SOUP

FILLING:

¾ lb lean ground pork
1 C fresh or frozen shrimp, shelled
    and chopped
1 T soy sauce
½ tsp garlic powder
½ tsp salt

½ T dry sherry
1 C or 6 oz can water chestnuts,
    minced
1 lb wonton wrappers
1 egg, beaten

Combine soy sauce, sherry, garlic powder and salt with ground pork, shrimp and water chestnuts in a large bowl and set aside. Put almost a teaspoon of filling just off-center on wonton wrapper. Fold like a nurse's cap and seal with beaten egg.

Boil 4 quarts of water in a large pot. Put ½ of the filled wontons into the boiling water and cook for 5 minutes on medium heat with the cover on. When the wontons float to the top, the meat is cooked. Remove and gently drain in cold running water for a minute or two. Add more water to the pot, if necessary, and bring to a boil. Cook the second batch of wontons in the same manner. Wontons can be stored in a tight container in the freezer for future use.

Yield: 64 wontons

SOUP:

46 oz can chicken broth or homemade
    chicken broth
½ C Chinese black mushrooms
    (soaked in hot water for 1 hr and
    then shredded or 1 C fresh
    Shitake mushrooms, thinly sliced)

½ can water (using same can)
2 to 3 C bok choy, very thinly
    sliced
Few drops sesame oil
4 to 5 scallions, sliced

Place chicken broth, water and mushrooms in a large soup pot and boil. Reduce heat and simmer for another 20 minutes to bring out the flavor of the mushrooms. Add bok choy and again bring to a quick boil. Add cooked wontons to the soup and turn off the heat. Add the sesame oil and scallions.

Hint: Finely sliced Chinese roast pork is an authentic garnish that may be added to the soup. The soup base is really enough for only half the wontons, so I usually freeze the other 32 wontons and keep them for another time when I just want to make the soup base. Don't be discouraged by the length of this recipe. It is very easy to make if you follow the directions carefully. Once you taste it and hear everyone's raves, you'll be glad you tried it!

CHILLED AVOCADO SOUP

2 13 to 14 oz cans
chicken broth, chilled
2 ripe avocados
Dash fresh lemon juice

2 T dry sherry
1 C sour cream, plain yogurt or
all purpose cream (optional)
Fresh dill, chopped (for garnish)

Remove the fat from the canned broth and place the broth in a blender or processor. Add the avocados, lemon juice and sherry. Blend well. Add sour cream, yogurt or all purpose cream. Garnish with chopped dill. Serve in chilled soup bowls or mugs.

Hint: This is a delicious cold soup that is very easy to make. It tastes best when made several hours in advance.

COLD CUCUMBER SOUP EMPRESS

1 qt buttermilk
2 C sour cream or plain yogurt
3 T parsley, finely chopped
1 tsp salt
1 cucumber, peeled

½ cucumber, unpeeled
Dash Tobasco sauce
¼ small onion, finely chopped
½ C sliced almonds, toasted

Chop the parsley and onion in a food processor, using the steel blade. Remove the seeds from the cucumbers and discard. Coarsely chop the cucumber in the processor. In a large bowl whisk together the buttermilk, sour cream or yogurt and spices. Add chopped cucumber, parsley and onion. Blend well. Chill for several hours or overnight. Serve the soup in chilled bowls, garnished with toasted sliced almonds.

Hint: Even if you don't like buttermilk, this is delicious and refreshing! A melon baller makes it easy to remove the seeds from the cucumbers. To toast the almonds, bake at 350˚for 3 to 4 minutes.

ICHYSSOISE

3 C potatoes, peeled and sliced	Salt and white pepper, to taste
3 C leeks (white only), sliced	½ to 1 C medium cream
1½ qt chicken broth or bouillon	2 to 3 T chives, chopped

Simmer the potatoes and leeks in the broth or bouillon for 40 to 50 minutes, or until tender. Puree in blender or food processor, using the steel blade. Add salt and pepper. Stir in the cream. Chill well. Serve in chilled bowls, garnished with chives.

Hint: Add more salt than you normally do because as the soup chills, it loses the taste of the salt. This is a very refreshing way to begin a spring or summer meal.

AZPACHO

6 very ripe tomatoes, peeled and chopped	1½ C tomato juice
1 medium cucumber, peeled, seeded and chopped	3 T olive or canola oil
	2 T vinegar
1 small onion, finely chopped	1 tsp salt, or to taste
1 small green pepper, finely chopped	Black pepper, to taste
1 clove garlic, minced	2 to 3 drops Tobasco sauce
	Croutons (for garnish)

Puree all ingredients except croutons in a blender or food processor. Serve in chilled soup bowls or mugs. Garnish with croutons.

Hint: To peel tomatoes, place them in boiling water for about 30 to 40 seconds. Remove and immediately plunge them into ice cold water. Using a sharp paring knife, peel off skins. Gazpacho is a very refreshing soup that I first tasted in Spain many years ago. It is very low in calories and fat and is a great way to use any surplus vegetables you may have from your garden.

CHILLED PEACH SOUP

10 large ripe peaches, peeled and
  quartered
½ C sugar
1 pt sour cream
½ C fresh lemon juice

½ C dry white wine
4 T orange juice concentrate
Additional peach slices,
  raspberries or blueberries
  (for garnish)

Blanch peaches in boiling water for 30 to 40 seconds. Plunge them into cold water; then peel off skins. Cut peaches into quarters and remove pits. Puree peaches and sugar in a blender or food processor, using steel blade. Add remaining ingredients except for garnish. Chill. Garnish with peach slices or berries.

Yield: 8 ¾-cup servings

Hint: This tastes best if made a day in advance of serving. Serve in chilled soup bowls or mugs. For a large crowd, increase the recipe accordingly and serve in chilled punch cups. You may substitute light sour cream or plain yogurt for the sour cream.

CREAM OF CANTALOUPE SOUP

2 cantaloupes
2 to 3 T fresh lemon and/or
  lime juice
3 T Coco Lopez or any canned
  sweetened coconut cream
3 T white wine
1½ T orange flavored liqueur

3 to 4 T cream
White pepper, to taste
Freshly grated nutmeg,
  to taste
Mint leaves or shredded coconut,
  for garnish

Cut cantaloupes in half. Scoop out and discard seeds. Remove flesh and puree in a food processor or blender until very smooth. Pour into a bowl. Fold in all remaining ingredients. Chill well. Garnish with fresh mint leaves or shredded coconut.

Hint: This is very refreshing on a hot summer day. For a large group, serve it in punch cups instead of soup bowls.

33

TWO MELON SOUP

1 small very ripe cantaloupe, peeled, seeded and chopped
2 T fresh lemon juice
½ very ripe honeydew, peeled, seeded and chopped

3 T fresh lime juice
1½ tsp fresh mint, minced
Few mint sprigs, for garnish
Sour cream, for garnish (optional)

Puree cantaloupe in food processor or blender with lemon juice until smooth. Puree honeydew, lime juice and chopped mint the same way. Chill, covered, for at least 3 hours. Pour equal amounts of each puree, (using both hands at the same time) into each half of chilled bowls. Garnish with sour cream and mint.

Hint: This is such an unusual and pretty soup to serve because half of the bowl is orange and half is green. Also, the soup is refreshing and low in calories.

34

Breads

APPLE BREAD

1 C canola oil
3 eggs
2 C sugar
1 tsp vanilla
1 tsp cinnamon
1 tsp salt

1 tsp baking soda
3 C apples, finely diced
3 C flour
1 to 2 T sugar, for sprinkling
 on baked bread

Combine oil, eggs, sugar and vanilla. Sift flour with cinnamon, salt, and baking soda. Add to egg mixture. Fold in apples. Pour batter into 2 greased 8"x4" loaf pans. Bake 50 to 60 minutes at 300° until a toothpick, inserted in the center, comes out clean. While hot, sprinkle with sugar and as soon as it can be handled, remove it from the pan. Cool on a wire rack and then wrap the loaves in foil.

Yield: 2 loaves

Hint: This bread is delicious for breakfast or brunch. It freezes well.

APPLE PUMPKIN BREAD

¼ C butter or margarine, melted
¼ C canola oil
¾ C sugar
1 egg
1 C pumpkin puree, fresh or canned
1 C unpeeled apple, grated (1 medium) chopped
2 C flour

1 tsp baking soda
½ tsp baking powder
1 tsp cinnamon
¼ tsp salt (optional)
½ C raisins and/or ½ C nuts, chopped

TOPPING:

2 T butter or margarine
2 T sugar

2 T flour
½ tsp cinnamon

In a large bowl combine butter or margarine, oil, sugar, egg, pumpkin and apple. In a small bowl mix remaining ingredients except topping. Combine both mixtures and beat just until well moistened. Pour into a greased 9"x5" loaf pan. Combine topping ingredients until it resembles coarse meal. Sprinkle on top of loaf. Bake at 350° for 45 to 50 minutes or until a toothpick, inserted in center, comes out clean.

Hint: This is a moist, delicious bread that is high in fiber. It is a good way to use fresh pumpkin. It freezes well.

Yield: 1 loaf

DATE-APRICOT BREAD

1 C (4 oz) dates, chopped
1 C (4 oz) apricots, chopped
2 tsp baking soda
1½ C sugar
2 T butter or margarine

1¾ C boiling water
2 eggs, beaten
2½ C flour
1 C walnuts, chopped

Pour boiling water over first 5 ingredients. Add eggs, flour and walnuts and mix thoroughly. Pour into a greased 9"x5" loaf pan and let stand 15 minutes before baking. Bake at 350° for 50 to 60 minutes, or until a toothpick, inserted in the center, comes out clean.

Hint: Instead of using 1 (9"x5") loaf pan, you may use 3 mini-loaf pans (3"x6") or 1 (8½"x4½") loaf and 1 (3"x6") mini-pan. Reduce baking time accordingly. This bread freezes well and makes a wonderful gift.

DATE NUT BREAD

8 oz dates, chopped
1½ C boiling water
1¾ C sugar
3 C flour

1 C walnuts, chopped
2 T butter or margarine
2 tsp baking soda
2 eggs, beaten

Place dates and butter or margarine in a bowl. Pour boiling water over this and then let it sit until cool. Add beaten eggs and remaining ingredients. Bake in 2 greased 9"x5" loaf pans at 350° for 40 to 45 minutes, or until a toothpick, inserted in the center, comes out clean.

Yield: 2 loaves

Hint: This is an exceptionally moist and tasty bread that is delicious served with cream cheese or Orange Butter (pg.44). If you make this in the fall, you can carve out a mini-pumpkin, fill it with cream cheese, and serve it next to the bread. The bread freezes well, so you might like to keep one loaf in the freezer for unexpected guests or to give as a gift.

BANANA BREAD

1½ C flour
¾ tsp baking soda
½ tsp salt
¾ C butter or margarine
1½ C sugar
2 eggs

¼ C buttermilk, plain
  yogurt or sour milk
1 C very ripe bananas, mashed
  (2 medium)
2 tsp vanilla
1 C walnuts, chopped (optional)

Combine flour, baking soda and salt and set aside. Cream butter or margarine with sugar until fluffy. Add eggs and buttermilk, yogurt or sour milk and mix well. Add flour mixture alternately with bananas, beginning and ending with flour. Stir in vanilla and nuts. Bake in a greased 9"x5" loaf pan at 350° for 1 hour, or 2 (3"x6") mini-loaf pans at 350° for 45 to 50 minutes, or until a toothpick, inserted in the center, comes out clean.

Hint: With the rising cost of bananas, it's a shame to throw out overripe ones. This is a great way to use them! This bread freezes well. Also, if a recipe calls for buttermilk or sour milk, you can substitute plain yogurt or make sour milk by doing the following: Start with 1 cup milk. Remove 1 tablespoon milk and replace it with 1 tablespoon white vinegar or 1 tablespoon lemon juice. Stir and allow to stand for 10 to 15 minutes, or until slightly thickened.

LEMON BREAD

1 C sugar	1½ C flour
5 T butter or margarine	1 tsp baking powder
2 eggs	Rind of 1 lemon, grated
½ C milk	½ C walnuts or
½ tsp salt	pistachios, chopped

Cream butter or margarine and sugar until fluffy. Beat in eggs. Add milk and mix well. Sift dry ingredients together, add to batter and beat until smooth. Add lemon rind and nuts. Pour into a greased 9"x5" loaf pan and bake at 325° for 45 to 50 minutes.

Yield: 1 loaf

GLAZE:

Juice of 1 lemon   ⅓ C sugar

While bread is baking, mix lemon juice and sugar until sugar dissolves. Spoon glaze over hot bread before removing it from the pan. Continue until bread absorbs all the glaze. Cool before removing from the pan.

Hint: *This bread is delicious toasted and buttered. It may also be thinly sliced, buttered and made into dainty sandwiches. For tea-size sandwiches, bake in empty 6 ounce juice cans that have been greased and filled three-quarters full of batter. You may also use two mini-loaf pans (3"x6") and bake for less time. This bread freezes well and makes a wonderful gift.*

CHILI CORN BREAD

1 C butter or margarine	1 C Cheddar or Monterey Jack
¾ C sugar	cheese, shredded
4 eggs	1 C yellow cornmeal
4 oz can chopped green chilies	4 tsp baking powder
16 oz can cream style corn	½ tsp salt
1 C flour	

Cream butter or margarine and sugar. Add eggs, one at a time. Add chilies, corn and cheese; mix well. Sift flour, cornmeal and baking powder together; add to mixture. Add salt, to taste. Blend well. Pour into a greased 9"x13" pan. Place in a 350° preheated oven and immediately reduce heat to 300°. Bake 45 to 50 minutes. Cut into squares. Serve warm.

Hint: *This is a nice accompaniment to chili, beef stew or a hearty soup.*

38

IRISH BREAD

2½ C flour
½ tsp salt
2 tsp baking powder
½ tsp baking soda
¼ C butter or margarine
½ C sugar
1 egg

1½ C buttermilk or plain yogurt
⅓ C raisins
⅓ C currants
1 to 2 T caraway seeds, or to taste
2 tsp mixture of cinnamon and
    sugar

Sift together flour, salt, baking powder and baking soda. Set aside. Cream butter or margarine and sugar until fluffy. Add egg and buttermilk or yogurt. By hand, mix in dry ingredients until moistened. Add raisins, currants and caraway seeds. Pour into a greased 1½ quart round casserole dish or an 8-inch round cake pan. Sprinkle with cinnamon and sugar mixture. Bake at 375° for 30 minutes. Reduce oven temperature to 325° and bake for 20 to 25 more minutes or until a toothpick, inserted in the center, comes out clean. Remove from the pan immediately and cool on a wire rack.

Yield: 1 loaf

Hint: This bread was one of the most requested recipes from my television show. It seemed as if everyone, Irish or not, wrote in for it! It's a delicious bread that goes well with any meal, any time of the year. It freezes well. If you don't have currants, which look like tiny raisins, use all raisins.

ENGLISH MUFFIN BREAD

6 C flour
2 pkgs dry yeast
1 T sugar
2 tsp salt
¼ tsp baking soda

2 T orange rind, grated
2 C milk
½ C water
Cornmeal

Combine 3 cups flour, yeast, sugar, salt, baking soda and orange rind. Heat milk and water until very warm, approximately 115° to 120°. Do not boil. Add to dry ingredients and beat well. Stir in remaining flour to make a stiff batter. Spoon into 2 9"x5" loaf pans that have been greased and sprinkled with cornmeal. Sprinkle tops of loaves with cornmeal. Cover with a towel. Let rise in warm place for about 45 minutes. A perfect place for allowing the dough to rise is in an oven that has been turned on to 200° for 5 minutes and then shut off and closed. After the dough has risen, bake at 400° for 25 minutes. Remove from pans immediately and cool on a wire rack.

Yield: 2 loaves

Hint: This is a delicious bread that contains no fat or eggs! Although working with yeast sometimes frightens people, it really is so easy to make if you follow these instructions carefully. This bread freezes well.

ERSATILE MUFFINS

1½ C flour
½ C sugar
½ tsp salt
2 tsp baking powder

¼ C canola oil
1 egg
½ C milk

Combine dry ingredients. Add oil, egg and milk and mix just until blended. Do not overmix. Add one of the following fruit fillings. Bake at 400° in greased muffin tins for 20 minutes. Cool in pan for 10 minutes before removing to a wire rack.

Yield: 1 dozen small muffins (If larger muffins are desired, fill only 8 to 10 muffin cups.)

FILLING VARIATIONS:

Apple
2 C apples, diced
1 tsp cinnamon

Topping
½ tsp cinnamon
¼ C brown sugar
¼ C walnuts, chopped

Fold apples and cinnamon into batter and sprinkle with topping.

Apple-Pineapple
8 oz crushed pineapple, drained
1 apple, diced
½ tsp cinnamon

Topping same as apple

Fold in fruit and cinnamon and sprinkle with topping.

Banana-Nut
1 large or 2 small bananas, mashed
½ C walnuts, chopped

Fold bananas and nuts into the batter.

Blueberry
1 C blueberries
Dash cinnamon

Fold in blueberries and cinnamon and sprinkle tops with sugar.

Pumpkin
1 C pumpkin puree
½ tsp cinnamon
½ tsp nutmeg
½ C walnuts, chopped or ½ C raisins

Fold pumpkin, spices and nuts or raisins into the batter.

Hint: *This recipe is from a bed and breakfast we stayed at in Maine. Everyone loves the muffins and can't wait to get up in the morning to see what kind are being served that day!*

Cinnamon Rolls

1 pkg dry yeast
¼ C warm water (105° to 115°)
4 C flour
¾ C sugar, divided
1 C lukewarm milk, scalded and cooled

1 tsp salt
1 C butter or margarine, softened
3 egg yolks, beaten
1½ tsp cinnamon
2 T butter or margarine, melted

Dissolve yeast in warm water. Combine flour, ¼ cup sugar and salt in a large bowl. Cut in 1 cup butter or margarine with a pastry fork until it looks like cornmeal. Stir in yeast, egg yolks and milk. Mix until dough is smooth. Cover and refrigerate at least 8 hours. Grease 24 muffin tins. Turn half the dough onto a floured surface and roll into a rectangle 10"x12". Brush with melted butter or margarine. Mix ½ cup sugar and the cinnamon and sprinkle half of it over the rectangle. Roll up like a jellyroll beginning at wide side. Pinch edges to seal. Cut into 1-inch slices and lay slices on their sides so that cut sides face up and place in greased muffin tins. Cover and let rise until double, 1 to 1½ hours. Bake at 375° for 10 to 15 minutes or until golden. While warm, frost with glaze.

Yield: 24 rolls

GLAZE:

1½ C confectioners' sugar, sifted
2 T butter or margarine, softened

1½ tsp vanilla
1 to 2 T hot water

Combine butter or margarine and sugar. Blend well. Add vanilla and hot water and beat until smooth.

Hint: This is a recipe from one of the first cooking series I taught. Although today many people don't often have the time to make their own rolls, it is fun to do occasionally, or for special events. This is cool rise dough so you can make it a day ahead, let it rise overnight in the refrigerator and bake it off the next day. This really reduces the usual rising time that deters many people from working with yeast. These rolls are so delectable that the raves you receive will make you want to make them again and again! If you have leftovers, they freeze well. If you like, add raisins and chopped nuts to the sugar and cinnamon mixture.

41

CREAM CHEESE BRAIDS

1 C sour cream	2 pkgs dry yeast
½ C sugar	½ C warm water (105° to 115°)
1 tsp salt	2 eggs, beaten
½ C butter or margarine, melted	4 C flour

Heat sour cream over low heat; stir in sugar, salt and butter or margarine. Cool to lukewarm. Sprinkle yeast over warm water in a large mixing bowl, stirring until yeast dissolves. Add sour cream mixture, eggs and flour. Mix well. Cover tightly; refrigerate overnight. The next day, divide dough into four equal parts; roll out each part on a well-floured board into a 12"x8" rectangle. Spread a quarter of Cream Cheese Filling on each rectangle. Roll up jellyroll fashion, beginning at long sides. Pinch edges together and fold ends under slightly. Place the rolls seam side down. Slit each roll at 2-inch intervals two-thirds of the way through dough to resemble a braid. Cover and let rise in a warm place, free from drafts, until doubled in bulk, about 1 hour. Place on greased cookie sheets and bake at 375° for 12 to 15 minutes until almost golden. Spread with glaze while warm.

Yield: 4 12" loaves

CREAM CHEESE FILLING:

2 8 oz pkgs cream cheese, softened	⅛ tsp salt
¾ C sugar	2 tsp vanilla
1 egg, beaten	

Cream the cream cheese and sugar together in a small mixing bowl. Add egg, salt and vanilla. Mix well.

GLAZE:

2 C confectioners' sugar, sifted	2 tsp vanilla
4 T milk	

Combine all ingredients in a small bowl. Mix well.

Hint: Although this is one of the longest recipes in the book, I decided to include it due to popular demand. I taught how to make this bread in some of my cooking classes years ago and everyone loved it. It should be started a day ahead, so that it can be made in stages and is therefore, much easier to make than it sounds. For several holiday seasons, it was my traditional gift for teachers, school bus drivers and neighbors, so I thought I would share it with you. To give as a gift, wrap the braid tightly in foil, twist the ends and tie it with ribbons. The braid may be frozen and then defrosted and reheated slightly before serving. These braids should be warmed slightly before serving.

CALZONE

1 loaf frozen bread dough
or 1 lb pizza dough
4 oz Cheddar cheese, shredded
2 pkgs frozen chopped spinach or
broccoli, cooked and drained

4 oz Muenster cheese, thinly sliced
Garlic powder, salt and pepper
to taste
1 egg, beaten

Grease a 10½"x15½" jellyroll pan. Roll out dough or press it all over pan.
Spread Cheddar cheese over dough. Spread spinach on top and then cover
with slices of Muenster cheese. Sprinkle with spices. Turn cookie sheet
vertically and fold a third of dough closest to you up towards middle of pan.
Fold furthest third down onto that. Then turn whole "envelope" horizontally
onto pan so that it looks like one long loaf. Brush with beaten egg. Bake at
350˚ for 30 to 35 minutes, or until golden. Let stand 15 minutes. Cut into
slices.

*Hint: Broccoli, pepperoni, salami or any combinations of these and/or other
cheeses may be used as fillings for calzone. Pizza dough is often sold by the
pound in supermarkets or Italian bakeries.*

POPOVERS

2 eggs
1 C milk

1 C flour, sifted
½ tsp salt

Combine all ingredients in a mixer or food processor, using the steel blade,
just until smooth. Fill greased popover pans or custard cups three-quarters
full. If using muffin tins, grease and fill only 8 of them to the top. Bake at
450˚ for 20 minutes, reduce temperature to 375˚ and bake 5 to 10 minutes
longer, or until firm to the touch.

*Hint: To get really large popovers, use 6 greased ovenproof custard cups or
popover pans. For best results, popovers should be served immediately after
baking.*

43

ORANGE BUTTER

1 stick butter
1 T orange rind, finely grated

1 T frozen orange juice
    concentrate, defrosted

Combine all ingredients in a mixer or food processor, using steel or plastic blade, until smooth.

Hint: This butter is delicious on date nut, whole wheat or white bread. It keeps well in the refrigerator for at least a week.

HERB BUTTER

1 stick butter
2 tsp oregano
2 tsp parsley
2 tsp basil

2 tsp chives
1 clove garlic, finely minced
Salt, to taste
Squeeze of fresh lemon, to taste

Combine all ingredients in a mixer or food processor, using steel or plastic blade, until smooth. Spread on bread and place under broiler, if desired.

Hint: This butter is delicious on almost any kind of bread. Either dried or fresh herbs may be used. If using fresh, however, triple the amount of herbs because the ratio of fresh to dried herbs is always 3:1. It keeps well in the refrigerator for at least a week.

Salads and Jello Molds

CAESAR SALAD

SALAD:

2 heads Romaine lettuce
1 to 2 C croutons

¾ to 1 C Parmesan cheese, freshly grated

DRESSING:

1 C olive oil
1 garlic clove
Pinch cayenne pepper
2 to 3 drops Tobasco sauce

½ tsp sugar
1 egg
6 anchovy fillets, mashed
Juice of 1 large lemon

Wash and dry lettuce and tear into bite-size pieces. Chill until serving time. To make dressing, place oil in pint-size jar. Crush garlic clove and place in jar. Allow garlic to steep in oil for at least one day, if possible. Then add remaining ingredients. Cover jar and shake well. When ready to serve, place lettuce leaves in salad bowl. Sprinkle with Parmesan cheese and croutons. Pour dressing over mixture and toss.

Hint: Freshly grated Parmesan cheese makes all the difference in the world in this recipe. If you like, add even more Parmesan! It is also important, in this salad, as well as in every salad, to make sure the greens are dry, otherwise the dressing will slide off the greens and form a puddle in the bottom of the bowl.

MANDARIN SALAD

SALAD:

½ C sliced almonds
3 T sugar
½ head iceberg lettuce
½ head Romaine lettuce

1 C celery, chopped
2 scallions, chopped
11 oz can mandarin oranges, drained

DRESSING:

½ tsp salt
¼ C olive or canola oil
2 T sugar

2 T cider vinegar
Dash Tobasco sauce

In a small pan over medium heat cook almonds and sugar; stir constantly until almonds are coated and sugar is dissolved. Cool and store in an airtight container. Combine all dressing ingredients and chill. Tear lettuce into bite-size pieces and place in a large bowl. Add celery, scallions and oranges. Just befoe serving, add almonds and dressing and then toss.

Hint: When heating almonds and sugar, watch constantly so that they don't burn. The almonds may be glazed several days in advance and stored in a tin. The only problem is that they are so delicious that there may not be any left when you go to serve the salad! This salad has gotten rave reviews in many of my cooking classes and dinner parties!

SPINACH SALAD WITH CHUTNEY DRESSING

SALAD:

1 large bunch (or 2 10 oz bags)
fresh spinach
8 mushrooms, thinly sliced
6 oz can water chestnuts, sliced

1 C fresh bean sprouts
2 scallions, sliced
Sesame seeds, toasted (for garnish)

CHUTNEY DRESSING:

¼ C wine vinegar
3 T mango chutney
1 clove garlic, minced
2 T Dijon mustard

2 tsp sugar
⅓ C canola oil
Salt and pepper, to taste

Wash, dry and trim the spinach. Add the mushrooms, scallions, bean sprouts and water chestnuts. Refrigerate all salad ingredients until they are ready to use. Combine all salad dressing ingredients, except oil, in a blender or food processor. With machine running, slowly pour in oil until the mixture becomes thick and smooth. Taste and adjust seasonings. Place in a covered container and refrigerate. Bring the dressing to room temperature 30 minutes before serving. Toss with the salad ingredients. Sprinkle with sesame seeds when ready to serve.

Hint: The dressing may be made 1 to 2 days in advance. To toast the sesame seeds, bake in a 350° oven for 3 to 5 minutes, or until golden. Watch carefully or the seeds will burn!

CHICK PEA SALAD

SALAD:

2 19 or 20 oz cans chick peas
  (or garbanzo beans)
1 C tomatoes, peeled, seeded
  and chopped

¼ C pimentos, coarsely chopped
1 C red onion, finely chopped
2 T fresh parsley, minced

DRESSING:

1 T garlic, minced
Juice of one lemon
2 T olive or canola oil
1½ tsp fresh oregano, minced
  (or ½ tsp dried oregano)
½ tsp black pepper

1 tsp Dijon mustard
1½ T red wine vinegar
1 T fresh basil, minced
  or ½ T dried basil
Salt, to taste

Rinse chick peas under cold water. Drain them thoroughly and transfer them to a large mixing bowl. Add the tomatoes, pimentos, onion and parsley. Toss lightly. Prepare the dressing by mixing the garlic, mustard and lemon juice in a bowl. Add the wine vinegar and olive or canola oil; blend until smooth. Add the basil, oregano, salt and pepper. Mix. Add the dressing to the chick pea mixture and toss to coat.

Hint: This is an inexpensive, low fat, high protein salad. It keeps well for a few days and is very portable. It is one of my son's favorite snacks!

MARINATED ROASTED PEPPERS

8 peppers, green and red mixed
1 C olive or canola oil
¼ C vinegar
1 tsp salt, or to taste
Black pepper, to taste

½ tsp dry mustard
1 bay leaf
2 cloves garlic, crushed
1 tsp basil

Place peppers under the broiler, or over an open gas flame or an outdoor grill. Turn with long handled tongs as the skins blacken, exposing each side of peppers to the open flame. When thoroughly blackened, place them in a brown paper bag for 10 to 15 minutes. Then remove from bag and run them under cold running water and peel off all charred outer skins. Halve peeled peppers and remove the seeds. Cut them into quarters. Place them in a saucepan and then pour remaining ingredients over them. Simmer, covered, for 15 minutes. Cool in marinade. Serve, drained on a leaf of lettuce or toast, as an appetizer.

Hint: This is a great way to use peppers when your garden is overflowing with them. Yellow, orange and purple peppers may be combined with red and green peppers or substituted for them. This will keep in the refrigerator for a few weeks.

THREE BEAN SALAD

SALAD:

19 or 20 oz can chick peas, drained
or 16 oz can kidney beans, drained
16 oz can cut string beans, drained

16 oz can cut wax beans, drained
1 small onion, sliced in rounds
1 medium green pepper, diced

DRESSING:

¼ C canola or olive oil
½ C vinegar

½ C sugar

Combine oil, vinegar and sugar. Pour over beans, chick peas or kidney beans, onion and pepper. Marinate overnight.

Hint: This is a colorful and tasty salad. It is especially good when you've run out of fresh produce. The beans and chick peas are a good and inexpensive source of protein. This will keep in the refrigerator for several days.

CONFETTI POTATO SALAD

3½ lbs potatoes, unpeeled and
    quartered
1½ to 2 C mayonnaise
¼ C cider vinegar
1 T sugar
2 to 3 tsp salt, or to taste

½ tsp black pepper
2 C celery, diced
¾ C parsley, chopped
¾ C carrots, grated
2 T fresh dill or chives, finely
    chopped (optional)

Place potatoes and enough water to cover them in a large pot. Bring the water to a boil; lower heat and simmer until the potatoes are tender. Remove from heat and allow potatoes to cool just enough so you can easily handle them. Peel and slice the potatoes. Whisk together mayonnaise, vinegar, sugar, salt and pepper. Place potatoes, celery, onion, parsley and carrots in a large bowl. Fold in mayonnaise mixture. Add dill or chives, if desired. Chill for several hours or overnight before serving.

Hint: You may use low calorie, cholesterol free or fat free mayonnaise in this recipe. Adjust the amount of mayonnaise, salt and pepper to suit your own taste. To speed up the cooling time for the potatoes, drain them and fill the pot with cold water. The potatoes will cool down very quickly and peel easily.

CABBAGE AND NOODLE SALAD

SALAD:

3 oz pkg dried chicken flavored
    Oriental noodle soup
6 C green cabbage, shredded

4 scallions, chopped
½ C sunflower kernels, toasted
½ C sliced almonds, toasted

DRESSING:

Seasoning packet from soup
½ C canola oil
3 T vinegar

2 T sugar
Black pepper, to taste

Remove seasoning packet from noodle package and set aside. Crush noodles and combine with cabbage, scallions, sunflower kernels and almonds and place in a large bowl. Whisk seasoning packet mixture with oil, vinegar, sugar and pepper. Pour this dressing over the cabbage mixture and toss gently. Cover and refrigerate for several hours or overnight before serving.

Hint: This is a unique and delicious salad that is high in fiber. To toast the almonds and sunflower kernels, bake them in a 350° oven for about 3 minutes, checking carefully so they don't burn.

TABBOULI

SALAD:

1 C bulghur wheat or cracked wheat
1½ C cold water
½ C fresh mint, chopped
1 C fresh parsley, chopped

½ C scallions, chopped
2 medium tomatoes, seeded and chopped

DRESSING:

¼ C fresh lemon juice
¼ to ⅓ C olive oil

Salt and pepper, to taste

Place the bulghur wheat in a large bowl and cover with cold water. Let stand for 1 hour or until the water is absorbed. Fluff up with a fork. Add chopped vegetables and dressing. This is great served with small Romaine lettuce leaves used as scoopers or as a filling for fresh tomatoes, peppers or pita bread.

Hint: The main ingredient for tabbouli, a Middle Eastern salad or appetizer, is bulghur, a healthy grain that has a nutty flavor. Bulghur may be purchased in health food stores or in supermarkets near the rice. Tabbouli tastes best if made a few hours, or even a day, before serving.

CABBAGE-CUCUMBER SALAD

SALAD:

1 medium green cabbage, shredded
1 medium Spanish or Vidalia onion*, thinly sliced
2 carrots, grated

1 green pepper, diced
2 cucumbers (with skin), thinly sliced

DRESSING:

½ C white vinegar
2 to 3 tsp salt, or to taste
½ C sugar

Black pepper, to taste
2 T canola oil
¼ C water

Whisk dressing ingredients together and pour over vegetables. Mix well. Marinate in refrigerator for several hours, overnight, or up to 2 days before serving.

Hint: This salad is very low in fat and calories and very high in fiber. It's great to bring to a picnic or barbeque because it holds up well at room temperature for several hours. It will still taste good 4 to 5 days after it was made.

* Spanish onions are the large variety that are a little sweeter than regular-sized yellow onions. When Vidalia onions are in season, they add a nice flavor. In a pinch, however, any onion will do.

EUROPEAN STYLE CUCUMBER SALAD

4 cucumbers, peeled and thinly sliced
1 small onion, thinly sliced
1 C white vinegar

½ C water
¾ C sugar
1 T fresh dill, finely minced

Place cucumbers and onion slices in a bowl. Combine remaining ingredients in a saucepan. Bring to a boil; pour over cucumber and onion slices. Refrigerate.

Hint: This tastes best when eaten the same day it has been prepared. Slicing the cucumber and onion are very easy if you use the slicing disc of a food processor. This salad is very refreshing, especially on a hot summer day.

ORIENTAL CUCUMBER SALAD

3 cucumbers
1 tsp salt (for sprinkling over cucumbers)
3 T wine vinegar

3 T soy sauce
3 T sugar
1 T sesame oil

Peel cucumbers and slice them very thinly. Place the slices in a colander, sprinkle with salt, and let stand for 20 minutes. Drain and transfer to a bowl. Combine wine vinegar, soy sauce, sugar and sesame oil and pour over the drained cucumbers. Mix well. Refrigerate for several hours, stirring occasionally. Serve cold.

Hint: This is a delicious salad, especially for a Chinese meal, or to accompany a barbeque featuring grilled steak or chicken teriyaki.

ORIENTAL BROCCOLI SALAD

1½ to 2 lbs fresh broccoli
2 T soy sauce

1 T sesame oil
1½ tsp sugar

Cut broccoli and separate stems from flowerettes. Slice stems into rounds or strips. Steam stems and flowerettes separately in a vegetable steamer or microwave just until broccoli turns bright green. Immediately plunge into cold water to stop the cooking. Cool. Combine remaining ingredients and pour over the broccoli. Refrigerate for several hours before serving, tossing occasionally.

Hint: This is a good accompaniment to a Chinese meal or for a barbeque featuring grilled steak or chicken.

MARINATED TOMATO SALAD

SALAD:

3 large ripe tomatoes, sliced
¼ tsp freshly ground black
  pepper, or to taste
½ tsp salt, or to taste

3 T fresh parsley or
  basil, finely chopped
3 T red or white onion, chopped

DRESSING:

3 T olive oil
2 T red wine vinegar

½ tsp sugar

Layer tomato slices in a bowl, sprinkling salt and pepper over each layer.
Sprinkle with onions and parsley or basil. Combine dressing ingredients and
pour over the tomatoes. Gently toss. Cover and marinate for at least an hour
or up to 24 hours. Serve chilled or at room temperature.

*Hint: This salad is especially delicious using tomatoes picked from the vine or
anytime during peak tomato season.*

GREEK SALAD

SALAD:

1 small head lettuce
2 stalks celery, sliced
1 small cucumber, peeled and sliced
1 green pepper, cut into strips

1 tomato, cubed or
  12 cherry tomatoes
4 oz Feta cheese, crumbled
½ C black olives

DRESSING:

⅔ C olive oil
⅓ C wine vinegar
1 tsp salt, or to taste

¼ tsp pepper
1 garlic clove, minced
1 tsp oregano

Combine ingredients for dressing in a jar and shake well. Refrigerate until
serving time. Tear lettuce into bite-size pieces and place in a large salad
bowl. Add remaining vegetables and olives and toss. Sprinkle Feta cheese
over top. Just before serving, pour on dressing and toss. Serve with pita
bread halves.

*Hint: This dressing may be made a few days in advance and kept in the
refrigerator. This salad is perfect for a picnic because the dressing can be
brought in its original jar, the salad can be placed in a plastic bag or covered
serving bowl and the bread can be kept in a plastic bag. Just assemble at the
picnic table!*

PAGHETTI SALAD

SALAD:

8 oz spaghetti, cooked and drained
4 medium tomatoes, cut in chunks
1 cucumber, peeled and cut in chunks

1 onion, chopped
¼ C parsley, chopped
⅓ to ½ lb Feta cheese, crumbled

DRESSING:

¼ C olive oil
2 T fresh lemon juice
3 T wine vinegar
1 T sugar

1 T fresh basil, finely chopped
  or 1 tsp dried basil
¼ tsp pepper
  Dash Tobasco sauce

Combine ingredients for dressing and refrigerate for several hours or up to a few days ahead. Cook spaghetti and drain. Transfer to a large bowl. While spaghetti is still hot, mix with Feta cheese. Add tomatoes, cucumber, onion and parsley. Add dressing and toss.

Hint: If you find that Feta cheese is too salty, try the imported Feta from France. It is much creamier in texture and a lot less salty than domestic Feta. You may substitute 1 heaping tablespoon of dried parsley for the fresh parsley. The ratio between fresh to dried herbs is 3:1. You need three times as much of the fresh as dried. This salad is fantastic in late summer when fresh basil and native tomatoes are at their peak!

ALAD NICOISE

SALAD:

8 to 10 red or new potatoes
2 T scallions, minced
2 T dry white wine or vermouth
3 T parsley, minced
1 to 2 heads Boston lettuce, washed and dried
2 6½ oz cans white tuna, drained
½ C black olives

3 to 4 tomatoes, quartered, or 12 cherry tomatoes
3 to 4 hard boiled eggs, peeled and quartered
1 small can anchovy fillets, drained
½ lb green beans drained
Salt and pepper, to taste

VINAIGRETTE DRESSING:

⅔ C olive oil
3 T wine vinegar
1 T fresh lemon juice

1 to 2 T Dijon mustard (or ½ tsp dry mustard)
Salt and pepper, to taste

Combine vinaigrette ingredients in a jar and shake well. Set aside. Steam potatoes until tender, about 15 to 20 minutes. Peel, if desired, and slice. Toss with wine or vermouth, scallions, salt and pepper. Allow to sit for a few minutes, or until liquid and seasonings have been absorbed. Toss again with about ½ C vinaigrette and parsley. Blanch green beans in boiling water for 3 to 4 minutes. Immediately plunge into ice water to stop the cooking. Drain and chill. Toss lettuce with a few tablespoons of the vinaigrette dressing and arrange on a large platter. Arrange tuna in center of platter and place potato salad, beans, tomatoes, eggs, etc. in a decorative design around it. Serve with extra dressing on the side.

Hint: This salad makes a wonderful spur of the moment meal to serve on the patio or porch during the dog days of summer. Potato salad from a deli may be substituted for the potato salad in this recipe. Hard boiled eggs, tomatoes and olives may be purchased at a salad bar. The only thing in this recipe that needs to be cooked are the green beans.

ORIENTAL CHICKEN SALAD WITH ALMONDS

SALAD:

3 C cooked chicken, shredded
1 C scallions, sliced
½ lb pea pods, blanched
1 C slivered almonds, toasted
½ red pepper, cubed

DRESSING:

¼ C prepared teriyaki sauce
3 T fresh lemon juice
¼ C peanut or canola oil
¼ tsp crushed red pepper
flakes (optional)

Combine ingredients for dressing. Then combine salad ingredients and pour dressing on top. Toss well.

Hint: The flavor of this dressing will vary according to the brand of teriyaki sauce used. Make the dressing a couple of days in advance and keep in the refrigerator.

FRUITED TURKEY OR CHICKEN SALAD

1½ C (½ lb) turkey or
chicken, cut into ½" cubes
1 C green grapes
⅓ C (½ can) water chestnuts,
drained and chopped
11 oz can mandarin oranges,
drained
1 tsp soy sauce
½ C mayonnaise
½ tsp curry powder, or to taste

Combine soy sauce, mayonnaise and curry powder. Fold in turkey or chicken, grapes, water chestnuts and oranges.

Hint: This recipe is great for using leftover turkey or chicken. If, however, your don't have any cooked turkey or chicken, a shortcut is to buy some cooked turkey breast at a deli and have it sliced into ½-inch slices. Then cut it into cubes to make the salad. This salad is nice to serve for a shower, luncheon or brunch. It looks especially lovely when served in a round pumpernickel bread that has been hollowed out.

RIENTAL WONTON SALAD

SALAD:

8 to 10 wonton skins
1 head iceberg lettuce, shredded
1 C celery, thinly sliced
1 C scallions, thinly sliced
1 red pepper, thinly sliced

3 whole chicken breasts, cooked and shredded
2 T sesame seeds, toasted
2 T peanuts, toasted and ground

DRESSING:

¼ C peanut or canola oil
3 T rice wine vinegar or white rice vinegar
2 T sugar

1 T sesame oil
½ tsp salt
½ tsp black pepper

Cut wonton skins into ½-inch strips and deep-fry until golden, about 1 minute. Remove from wok with a slotted spoon. Drain well on paper towels. Combine dressing ingredients in a jar. Shake well. Arrange lettuce on a platter. Pour dressing over vegetables and chicken; place over lettuce. Sprinkle with sesame seeds, peanuts and fried wonton strips.

Hint: Rice wine vinegar (sometimes called white rice vinegar) and sesame oil are found in the oriental section of most supermarkets, or in oriental markets. This is a very light and fresh tasting salad. Although it is oriental, it has none of the soy sauce most commonly found in oriental dishes. The dressing may be made a few days in advance. Leftover chicken may be used or you may poach the chicken breasts on top of the stove or in the microwave. Chicken will be easier to shred while still warm. The peanuts and sesame seeds may be toasted at 350° for 3 to 5 minutes. Then grind the peanuts in a blender or food processor.

MEXICAN TACO SALAD

1 lb lean ground beef, turkey or chicken
1¼ oz pkg (orless) taco seasoning mix
1 bunch scallions, chopped
1 head iceberg lettuce, shredded
3 tomatoes, diced

8 oz sharp Cheddar cheese, shredded
4 to 5 oz nacho chips, broken into small pieces
6 to 8 oz bottled salad dressing such as French, Catalina, or Catalina Nonfat

Brown beef, turkey or chicken, stirring to crumble; pour off excess fat. Add taco mix. Line a large salad bowl with lettuce, and top with beef, scallions and tomatoes. Sprinkle with cheese and crumbled nacho chips. Toss with enough dressing, to taste. If desired, serve with pita bread.

Hint: To cut down on the fat of a traditional taco salad, use ground turkey or chicken, instead of beef, low fat cheese and low fat or nonfat salad dressing. This makes a wonderful lunch or supper, especially on a hot summer day. It makes a real hit with people of all ages!

SALMON PASTA SALAD

SALAD:

8 oz rotini (twist pasta)
15 or 16 oz can salmon
4 to 5 scallions, chopped
¼ C parsley, chopped

2 to 3 T dill, chopped
4 stalks celery, diced
1 red or green pepper, diced

DRESSING:

¾ C mayonnaise
2 T fresh lemon juice
1 tsp prepared mustard

½ tsp celery seed
½ tsp salt, or to taste
¼ tsp black pepper

Drain and flake salmon. Combine all ingredients for dressing and mix with salmon. Cook, drain and cool pasta. In a large bowl, combine salmon mixture, vegetables and pasta. Mix well. Chill until serving time. Serve with a green salad or on individual plates that have been lined with lettuce.

Hint: You can use fresh cooked salmon instead of canned. Also, you may feel that you don't want to buy fresh parsley and dill just for this recipe. However, here's a tip here on how to process and keep it in your freezer so when you just need a little bit of dill or parsley, or any fresh herb, it will be easily available. Wash and dry the parsley and dill very thoroughly. Then chop it by hand or with the steel blade of your food processor. Use what you need immediately and then freeze the rest in a small freezer bag or plastic container. Then for future recipes, you can take out the amount you need. Herbs keep in the freezer for months.

THAI SEAFOOD SALAD

SALAD:

12 oz lobster, crab or
imitation crabmeat (surimi)
1 red or green pepper, chopped
1 cucumber, peeled and sliced
4 scallions, sliced
Lettuce

DRESSING:

2 T peanut butter
3 T soy sauce
⅓ C canola or peanut oil
4 tsp cider vinegar
2 tsp sugar
½ tsp red pepper flakes
(optional)

Combine seafood, pepper, cucumber and scallions. In a blender or food processor using steel blade, combine all dressing ingredients and blend until smooth. Toss with the seafood mixture. Place on a lettuce-lined platter.

Hint: If you are feeling affluent, use lobster or crab. However, this salad also tastes wonderful with surimi, or imitation crabmeat. The dressing may be made 1 to 2 days in advance.

CRAB AND PINEAPPLE SALAD

SALAD:

1 head green leaf lettuce,
washed and dried
1 lb lump crabmeat or imitation
crabmeat (surimi)
1 C cooked rice
1 C pineapple chunks
2 apples, cored and diced
3 T dill, minced
Few sprigs fresh dill, for garnish

DRESSING:

¾ C mayonnaise
2 T pineapple juice
1 T lemon juice
½ tsp paprika
Salt and pepper, to taste

Line a platter with lettuce. Combine remaining ingredients except dressing and mound on platter. Combine dressing ingredients and pour over crab mixture. Toss just before serving.

Hint: This is an unusually tasty flavor combination. The dressing and rice can be made a couple of days in advance which makes this easy to complete at the last minute. Drizzle some fresh lemon juice over the apple slices to prevent them from discoloring.

ENGLISH TEA ROOM SALAD DRESSING

1 C sugar   1 tsp celery seed
½ C vinegar   1 tsp salt
½ C canola oil   ½ tsp onion powder

Combine all ingredients and mix well. Chill for at least a few hours before serving. This dressing can be made a few days in advance.

Hint: This recipe is from a wonderful restaurant called the English Tea Room. It was a landmark on Newbury Street in Boston for many years. They were known for their salad, which was brought to the table family style, as well as for their huge meals that were "very cheap" as we used to say in our student days. The restaurant is no longer in existence, much to many people's dismay. Hopefully this recipe will bring back fond memories to many people when they taste this salad dressing!

BLUE CHEESE SALAD DRESSING

1 C Blue cheese, crumbled   1 T fresh lemon juice
1 clove garlic, finely minced   ⅔ C canola oil
1 T Worcestershire sauce   2 T white vinegar

In a blender or food processor, using the steel blade, combine everything but the oil. Then pour the oil slowly through the feed tube and process until thick and creamy.

Hint: If you don't have a blender or processor just shake all the ingredients together in a jar. Roquefort cheese may be used instead of Blue cheese. When refrigerated, this dressing solidifies and may be used as a spread on crackers. However, to use as a dressing, bring it to room temperature before serving.

PINEAPPLE LIME JELLO MOLD

6 oz lime jello
1 C boiling water
1 pt sour cream
⅓ C walnuts, chopped

20 oz can crushed pineapple, undrained
¼ C maraschino cherries, chopped (optional)

Dissolve jello in boiling water. Pour jello into sour cream and mix well. (Don't put sour cream into jello; it will become lumpy.) Stir in walnuts, pineapple and cherries, if desired. Pour into a 6-cup jello mold. Refrigerate several hours before serving. This may be made a day in advance.

Hint: This jello can serve as a salad with almost any entree.

CRANBERRY JELLO MOLD

6 oz pkg strawberry, raspberry or cherry jello
1 C boiling water
16 oz can whole cranberry sauce

20 oz can crushed pineapple
1 C celery, diced
1 C walnuts, chopped

Drain pineapple and reserve juice. Combine cranberry sauce with pineapple. Dissolve jello in boiling water. Add pineapple juice and mix well. Fold in celery, walnuts and cranberry mixture. Pour into a 6-cup jello mold. Chill until firm.

Hint: This is a unique way to serve cranberry sauce, especially with a turkey dinner. It may be made up to 2 days in advance and looks attractive when garnished with green grapes.

ORANGE SHERBET JELLO MOLD

6 oz pkg orange jello
2 11 oz cans mandarin oranges, drained

1 pt orange sherbet, softened
1 C boiling water
1 C cold orange juice

Dissolve jello in boiling water. Add orange juice and softened sherbet, mixing until smooth. Fold in oranges. Pour into a 6-cup jello mold. Refrigerate for several hours before serving. Garnish with fresh oranges and strawberries.

Hint: This jello mold is pretty, refreshing and may be made 1 to 2 days in advance.

ℛ IBBON JELLO MOLD

3 oz pkg lime jello
3 oz pkg lemon jello
3 oz pkg orange jello
3 oz pkg strawberry jello
1 C boiling water and ½ C cold
    water for each pkg jello

2 envelopes unflavored gelatin
½ C cold water
2 C milk
¾ C sugar
2 C sour cream
2 tsp vanilla

In separate bowls, dissolve each package of jello in 1 cup of boiling water and then add a ½ cup cold water. Mix well. Do not refrigerate. Dissolve unflavored gelatin in ½ C cold water and set aside. Bring milk just to the boiling point and add sugar, stirring until dissolved. Add reserved dissolved gelatin. Cool slightly. Combine sour cream and vanilla and add to milk mixture. Set aside. Do not refrigerate. This yields 4½ cups of white mixture. Use 1½ cups for each white layer in mold. To assemble mold, make green jello according to directions above. Pour into a 9"x13" oblong pan and refrigerate until set. Then pour 1½ cups white mixture over green layer and chill until set. Next make lemon jello as above and pour over white. Next layer will be white, etc. Continue layering with orange jello and then red as the top layer. It usually takes about 35 to 45 minutes per layer to gel. When layers are completed, chill until serving time. To serve, cut into squares and serve from that dish or place squares of the mold on another serving platter.

Hint: This mold is absolutely beautiful and a real conversation piece. Everyone comments on it and loves it. It is not at all difficult to make, however you have to be home for at least 4 to 5 hours in order to finish it. It can be made up to 2 days in advance.

Eggs and Cheese

YOGURT PANCAKES

1¼ C flour
1 T sugar
½ tsp salt, if desired
1 tsp baking powder
½ tsp baking soda
1¼ C plain yogurt or buttermilk
1 egg
2 T canola oil

Combine dry ingredients in a bowl. Add yogurt, egg and oil. Mix until just combined. Drop by tablespoons onto a slightly greased skillet and cook until tiny bubbles appear. Turn over and brown on the other side.

Yield: 14 pancakes

Hint: *Leftovers may be frozen and reheated in the toaster oven. You may add 1 cup diced apples, cranberries, blueberries, etc. to the batter before cooking. These pancakes are both low cholesterol and low fat if you use nonfat yogurt, egg substitute or 2 egg whites instead of a whole egg.*

PUFFY OVEN PANCAKE

½ C flour
½ C milk
2 eggs, slightly beaten
1 to 2 T butter or margarine
1 to 2 T confectioners' sugar
Juice of half a lemon
Jelly or jam (optional)

Preheat oven to 425°. Combine flour, milk and eggs. Beat lightly. Leave batter a little lumpy. Melt butter or margarine in a 10-inch skillet with an ovenproof handle or in a 9 or 10-inch pie plate in the oven. When melted, remove from the oven and pour the batter over it into the pan. Bake for 15 to 20 minutes or until golden and puffy. Sprinkle with confectioners' sugar and drizzle with lemon juice. Cut into wedges. Serve with jelly or jam, if desired.

Yield: 2 servings

Hint: *This has always been a favorite breakfast or brunch in our house. If your oven has a window in it, it is fun to watch the pancake "grow" as it bakes. When my sons were young, they were enthralled by watching! To double this recipe, use a 13"x9" pan and then cut the pancake into large squares.*

65

JELLYROLL PANCAKE

1 T canola oil	1 C milk
6 eggs	3 oz cream cheese, softened
Dash salt	½ C raspberry, black cherry
2 T sugar	apricot or jam of your choice
⅔ C flour	Confectioners' sugar

Preheat oven to 450°. Pour oil into a 10½"x15½"x1" jellyroll pan and place in oven while it is preheating. Beat the eggs and salt until light and fluffy. Combine the sugar and flour and add to eggs. Beat until smooth. Stir in milk and mix well. Remove the oiled pan from the oven and pour in the batter. Bake at 450° for 15 minutes, or until the pancake is puffy and golden. Remove from the oven and spread with cream cheese and jam of your choice. Beginning at long end of the pan, closest to you, pick up the pancake and roll it jellyroll fashion. Transfer it to an oblong serving platter and sprinkle with confectioners' sugar. Slice.

Yield: 6 portions

Hint: This is a favorite at our house for breakfast or brunch. It takes much less time to make than regular pancakes. Vary the flavor of jam to suit your taste.

POPPEL POPPEL

12 oz salami, chopped	12 eggs
6 scallions, chopped	½ tsp salt, or to taste
2 tomatoes, diced	½ tsp black pepper
1 large green pepper, chopped	6 oz smoked cheese, shredded

Beat eggs and seasonings. Add cheese, salami and vegetables. Pour into a greased 9"x13" baking dish and bake at 350° for 30 minutes or until egg mixture is set.

Hint: This is a fun way to serve eggs for a large crowd, especially because it can be made in advance and just popped into the oven. It's great for brunch or holiday breakfasts!

BAKED FRENCH TOAST WITH BLUEBERRY SAUCE

8 oz loaf French or Italian bread
4 eggs
½ C milk
¼ tsp baking powder
1 tsp vanilla
½ C sugar

1 tsp cinnamon
1 tsp cornstarch
5 C (approx. 1½ lbs) fresh
  or frozen blueberries
2 T melted butter or margarine
Confectioners' sugar

Slice the bread into 12 to 14 slices about ¾inch thick. Place on a 10½"x15½"x1" cookie sheet. Whisk eggs, milk, baking powder and vanilla together and slowly pour it over the bread, turning to coat the bread completely. Cover with plastic wrap and refrigerate for 1 to 2 hours, or overnight. Combine blueberries, cinnamon, sugar and cornstarch and place in a greased 9"x13" baking pan. Place bread, wettest side up, on the berry mixture. Wedge slices in tightly, cutting some pieces to fit, if necessary. Brush tops of bread with melted butter or margarine. Bake at 450° for 20 to 25 minutes or until the toast is golden and the berries are bubbling around the sides. Remove from the oven and sprinkle with confectioners' sugar. Let rest for 5 minutes before serving. To serve, lift toast onto plates and spoon blueberry sauce over it.

Hint: This is a delicious and easy to prepare breakfast or brunch dish, especially during blueberry season. If however, you use frozen berries, do not defrost them. You can start making this the night before by soaking the bread and finish assembling it in the morning. By the time the table is set and the coffee is made, the blueberry French toast will be ready to come out of the oven! You can use your imagination by trying strawberries, raspberries or sliced peaches or apples to vary the flavor of your Baked French Toast. Also, cholesterol free egg substitutes work very well in this recipe!

Mom's Noodle Pudding

16 oz wide noodles
1 pt sour cream
½ lb cream cheese
1 lb cottage cheese
4 eggs

Dash salt
6 T margarine, melted
Scant ½ C sugar
1 tsp vanilla
3 to 4 T brown sugar

Boil noodles and drain. Set aside. Combine all remaining ingredients except brown sugar. Add noodles to this egg mixture and fold well. Pour into a greased 9"x13" pan and sprinkle brown sugar over the top. Bake at 350° for 50 to 60 minutes, or until golden.

Hint: This is delicious for brunch or a light supper. It goes well with bagels and cream cheese!

Noodle Pudding with Apples

12 oz wide noodles
1 stick margarine
½ C sugar
½ C orange juice
4 eggs
½ C raisins

1 tsp cinnamon
16 oz can sliced apples or
6 fresh apples, sliced
¼ to ½ C bread crumbs
or corn flake crumbs

Cook noodles and drain well. Melt margarine in a 9"x13" pan. Remove 1½ to 2 tablespoons of melted margarine and set aside. Combine sugar, orange juice, eggs, raisins and cinnamon. Add noodles and mix well. Fold in canned apples or fresh apples that have been sauteed in a frying pan or cooked in a microwave until slightly tender. Pour noodle mixture into margarine-lined pan. Mix reserved margarine with bread or corn flake crumbs and sprinkle over top of pudding. Bake at 350° for 50 to 60 minutes, or until golden. Cut into squares.

Hint: This is delicious with pot roast, brisket or chicken. You can make it a day or two in advance.

BLINTZ SOUFFLE

4 eggs
1½ C sour cream
¼ C sugar
1 T orange juice

½ tsp salt
1 tsp vanilla
14 to 16 cheese blintzes

Blend all ingredients, except blintzes, in a blender or food processor. Allow this mixture to set for at least an hour or overnight. Then pour it over the still frozen blintzes that are neatly arranged in a greased 9"x13" pan. Bake at 325° for 1 hour, or until golden.

Hint: Serve with fresh strawberries or blueberries that have been pureed to make a sauce or use frozen berries in a syrup. This is great for brunch, especially for a big crowd because you can do all the work in advance. You can buy the blintzes already made, or if you are a purist, and have the time, you can make the blintzes.

CHEESE SOUFFLE

¼ C butter or margarine
1 C milk
Dash cayenne pepper
4 egg yolks
4 egg whites
¼ C flour

½ tsp salt, or to taste
4 oz Cheddar or Swiss cheese, shredded
2 tsp Parmesan cheese, finely grated

Grease a 1½ quart souffle dish and sprinkle with grated Parmesan cheese. In a saucepan melt butter or margarine, whisk in flour and seasonings. Add milk. Cook over medium heat, stirring until thick and bubbly. Remove from heat. Add shredded cheese and stir until melted. Separate eggs. Beat yolks until thick and lemon colored. Slowly add to cheese mixture, stirring constantly. Cool slightly. Beat egg whites and gradually pour yolk mixture over beaten whites and gently fold them together. Pour into prepared souffle dish. Bake at 400° for 25 minutes, without peeking!

Hint: For some reason, most people are afraid of souffles. However, if you follow this recipe exactly, you shouldn't have any problems. Be sure to allow the eggs to get to room temperature so that you'll get enough volume from the egg whites. Also, when separating the eggs, make sure that you don't get any yolk in the whites or the whites won't whip properly. Now you should be set to try it. Good luck!

𝒮HORT CUT SPINACH RICOTTA PIE

2 pkgs (10 oz) frozen chopped
  spinach, defrosted and
  drained well
8 oz Muenster cheese, sliced

8 oz ricotta cheese
½ tsp nutmeg
Dash pepper
2 eggs

Beat eggs. Add ricotta cheese, spinach, nutmeg and pepper. Grease a 9-inch pie plate and line with Muenster cheese slices. Fill with spinach mixture. Bake at 350º for 30 minutes.

Hint: *This freezes well, however if freezing, the baking time should be decreased to only 20 minutes. When reheating, do not defrost, but bake at 350° for only 10 to 15 minutes, or until hot. This may also be baked in an 8 or 9-inch square pan and cut into squares rather than wedges.*

ℱILO SPINACH PIE

2 10 oz pkgs frozen chopped spinach, defrosted and well drained
1 medium onion, chopped
1 T butter
½ lb Feta cheese
6 oz farmer's or pot cheese
3 eggs, lightly beaten
½ C bread crumbs
Salt, black pepper and nutmeg, to taste
⅓ to ½ box filo dough
1 stick butter, melted

Place the box of frozen filo dough in the refrigerator for several hours or a day before you use it. Saute onion in 1 tablespoon butter just until soft. Combine everything except filo dough and remaining butter in a food processor or blender. Open the box of filo and cut sheets at the halfway fold so that each piece will fit into an 8-inch square baking pan. Place five of these ½ sheets of dough on the bottom, buttering each one individually and layering one on top of another. Then place half of the filling mixture on top. Layer five more sheets of filo, buttering each one and then add the remaining filling on top. Place five more sheets of dough over that mixture, buttering each layer separately and fold the extra dough hanging over the sides on to the top of the pie. Brush butter on the top layer. Then bake at 375° for 30 to 40 minutes, or until golden. Wait 5 to 10 minutes before cutting.

Hint: Cut the pie into bite-size pieces to serve as hors d'oeuvres or cut into larger squares to serve as an entree. This pie is great for brunch or for a light supper. It may be made 1 to 2 days in advance or frozen. When working with filo dough, make sure that the dough not being used at the moment is kept covered with a damp towel so it won't dry out. Also, this is one of the few times that I recommend using butter as opposed to margarine. Since the filo is so delicate, it is advisable to use a goosefeather brush, which can be purchased at a gourmet shop, or a soft paint brush, for brushing the butter on the filo. If you use a stiff barbeque sauce brush, the dough is apt to tear. If you have always feared filo dough, this recipe is a good one to try!

Fish and Seafood

BAKED SCROD A LA RITZ

1 lb scrod fillets (blue cod, hake, etc.)
2 to 3 tsp fresh lemon juice
2 to 3 T melted butter or margarine

10 to 12 Ritz crackers, crushed into fine crumbs
2 to 3 T water

Season fillets with salt and pepper and sprinkle with lemon juice. Dip fillets in melted butter or margarine, then in Ritz cracker crumbs. Place on a baking sheet. Pour water in pan around the fish. Bake at 450° for 10 minutes per inch of fish thickness, then broil for 1 to 2 minutes or until golden, if desired.

Hint: This is a famous Boston scrod recipe. It works well with almost any fish fillet, even if you're not in Boston! Make your own Ritz cracker crumbs in the blender or food processor. If you want to jazz up this basic recipe, add grated Parmesan cheese to the cracker crumbs and use wine instead of water. The water or wine is the key to this recipe since it keeps the fish moist.

BAKED SCROD OR HADDOCK DIJONNAISE

1 lb scrod, haddock, hake, etc.
Garlic powder, to taste
1 T mayonnaise
½ tsp Dijon mustard
Dash pepper

1 to 2 T grated Parmesan cheese, (optional)
2 to 3 T seasoned bread crumbs
Lemon wedges, for garnish

Spray baking pan with nonstick cooking spray. Place fish on pan and spread with mixture of garlic powder, mayonnaise, Dijon mustard and pepper. Sprinkle with bread crumbs. Add Parmesan cheese, if desired. Bake at 450° for 10 minutes per inch of fish thickness, then broil for 1 to 2 minutes, or until golden. Garnish with lemon wedges.

Hint: This recipe is really just a guideline, not a precise formula. You can adjust the amounts and types of mayonnaise, mustard and bread crumbs to suit your taste.

FILLET OF SOLE SAUTE

1 lb fillet of sole
2 to 3 T flour
Salt and pepper, to taste

1 to 2 T fresh lemon juice
1 T olive oil
1 T butter

Combine flour, salt and pepper. Lightly dip sole into seasoned flour, shaking off the excess. Heat butter and olive oil in a frying pan. Saute fish fillets for approximately 1½ to 2 minutes per side. Squeeze a little fresh lemon juice directly into the frying pan and allow it to sizzle and reduce. Then swirl fish around in juice. Cook for one more minute or until fish is golden. Do not overcook.

Hint: Flounder, a flat fish similar to sole, also works well in this recipe. The secret to this recipe is adding the lemon juice while the fish is cooking, as opposed to squeezing it on after it is cooked.

LEMON FISH ROLL-UPS

2 lbs fillet of sole
⅓ C butter or margarine
⅓ C fresh lemon juice
½ tsp salt
¼ tsp pepper

1½ C cooked rice
1 C Cheddar cheese, shredded
10 oz pkg frozen chopped broccoli, defrosted and drained
Dash paprika

Melt butter or margarine and add lemon juice, salt and pepper. Combine rice, cheese and broccoli. Add ¼ cup butter mixture to rice mixture. Divide mixture by the number of pieces of fillet of sole. Place a mound of mixture on each fillet piece and roll up. Place seam side down in a greased oven-proof dish. Drizzle remaining lemon butter sauce over fillets. Sprinkle with paprika. Bake at 375° for 25 minutes.

Hint: Flounder, a flat fish similar to sole, also works well in this recipe. This may be prepared in advance and then baked right before serving. Serve with a yellow or orange vegetable and a salad.

MICROWAVE FILLET OF SOLE

1 lb fillet of sole
1 small onion, sliced
¼ C white wine

1 to 2 T Parmesan cheese
Salt and pepper, to taste
Lemon wedges, for garnish

Sprinkle fish fillets with salt and pepper. Roll up with darker side, where skin was removed, facing inside. Place fish in a microwave dish. Add wine and onions. Cover with waxed paper. Cook on high 4 minutes. Remove from oven and sprinkle a little Parmesan cheese on each fish roll. Let stand 1 minute before serving. Garnish with lemon wedges.

Hint: Flounder, a flat fish similar to sole, also works well in this recipe. This recipe contains no fat, except for that found in the Parmesan cheese, which can be omitted.

PECAN FILLET OF SOLE

1 lb fillet of sole or flounder
¼ C mayonnaise
¾ tsp lemon and pepper seasoning

½ tsp tarragon leaves
¼ C pecans, chopped

Combine mayonnaise and seasonings. Spread over fish. Sprinkle pecans over mixture. Bake at 450° for approximately 7 to 10 minutes, or until fish flakes.

Hint: Sole and flounder are both very thin, flat fish so they cook very quickly. Be sure not to overcook. Lemon and pepper seasoning is a combination found in the spice section of all supermarkets.

GRILLED HALIBUT, SALMON, SHARK, SWORDFISH OR TUNA STEAK

1 to 2 lbs fish steaks, 1" thick

MARINADE:

½ C olive or canola oil	1 shallot or 2 scallions,
¼ C dry white wine	finely chopped
1 clove garlic, finely chopped	2 tsp soy sauce
¼ tsp paprika	

Combine marinade ingredients. Place fish in marinade for at least 2 hours before grilling. Pre-oil or spray the grids of the grill with nonstick cooking spray to minimize sticking. Grill fish for approximately 5 to 6 minutes per side, or until done.

Hint: Fish should be cooked for a total of 10 minutes per inch of thickness.

GRILLED FISH IN FOIL

1½ lbs bluefish, scrod, haddock or sole fillets	1 to 2 carrots, grated or chopped
1 green, yellow or red pepper, chopped	1 to 2 T olive oil or melted margarine
1 small zucchini, grated or chopped	1 tsp fresh lemon juice
1 medium ripe tomato, chopped	1 tsp chopped parsley, dill or oregano

Cut a piece of heavy duty foil to approximately 12"x18". Grease lightly or spray with nonstick cooking spray. Combine vegetables and place on foil. Top with fish. Sprinkle with lemon juice, oil or melted margarine, chopped parsley, dill, basil or oregano, etc. Fold up foil to make a package. Place package on hot grill. Cook about 20 to 25 minutes, or until fish flakes.

Hint: While the fish is grilling, you can grill some sliced potatoes in another packet of foil. Just add sliced onions, salt, pepper and a little olive oil to the potatoes. Turn packet over every 5 minutes, cooking for a total of about 25 minutes. This way your entire dinner will be cooked on the grill. There will be no pans to wash and no kitchen to clean!

GRILLED OR BROILED SWORDFISH, TUNA, SHARK OR SALMON STEAK

1" to 1½" thick swordfish, tuna, shark or salmon steak

Mayonnaise
Lemon wedges, for garnish

If grilling outdoors, oil cooking grids or spray with nonstick cooking spray. Spread a thin coating of mayonnaise on one side of fish. Place coated side on grids or on broiling rack and cook for 5 to 6 minutes. Turn it over, spread with thin coating of mayonnaise and cook for the same length of time. Test for flakiness. If not cooked enough, continue cooking until just done. Do not overcook! Garnish with lemon wedges.

Hint: Reduced calorie or cholesterol free mayonnaise may be substituted for traditional mayonnaise. The mayonnaise helps the fish retain its natural moisture, however, it doesn't impart much flavor. If you'd like to add more flavor to the fish, mix some Dijon or honey mustard with the mayonnaise or try adding fresh dill or tarragon to it.

MARINATED SWORDFISH STEAKS OR KABOBS

2 lbs swordfish steaks or kabobs
⅔ C olive or canola oil
⅓ C fresh lemon juice

⅛ tsp dry mustard
1 tsp basil
Salt and pepper, to taste

Combine all ingredients, except swordfish, in a bowl or shake in a covered jar. Pour over swordfish steaks or kabobs and allow to marinate for 1 to 3 hours. Grill or broil for approximately 10 minutes per inch of thickness, turning over half way.

Hint: This marinade may also be used for salmon, shark or tuna steaks.

SALMON OR RAINBOW TROUT IN FOIL

1 lb salmon or rainbow trout fillets	1½ tsp Dijon mustard
1½ T olive oil	1½ T parsley, chopped
1½ T fresh lemon juice	

Whisk oil, lemon juice and mustard together. Cut fillets in half and place each half on a piece of foil approximately 12 inches square. Pour half of the lemon-oil mixture on top of each portion of fish. Sprinkle half the parsley on top of that. "Drugstore wrap"* fish in foil and place on a baking sheet. Bake at 450° for 15 to 18 minutes, or until salmon is cooked completely. Serve one packet per person. To prepare in advance, assemble packets several hours earlier in the day and refrigerate. Remove from refrigerator a half hour before placing them in the oven.

Hint: I have made this recipe in many cooking classes and demonstrations and people who have never tasted salmon before, or those who never liked it before, always raved about it. Cooked this way, the fish has a very delicate flavor. The added bonus is that it is a very healthy recipe!

*Bring two opposite ends of foil together and fold over tightly. Then seal the other two ends.

SALMON SAUTE

1 lb salmon fillet	2 T Parmesan cheese, or to taste
1 egg white	2 T olive oil
½ C seasoned bread crumbs	

Combine bread crumbs and cheese. Lightly beat egg white with a fork and dip both sides of salmon into it. Then dip into crumb mixture. Saute in olive oil over medium heat for approximately 5 to 6 minutes per side, or until salmon is cooked.

Hint: This is an unusual and easy way to prepare salmon.

POACHED SALMON WITH CUCUMBER SAUCE

3 salmon steaks (1 to 1½ lbs)   2 T fresh lemon juice
1½ tsp salt

Boil 1 quart water with the salt and lemon juice in a large skillet (a frying pan is perfect). Add salmon, reduce heat and cover. Simmer for 10 minutes. Remove salmon and allow to cool just enough to handle. Remove skin and outer layer of brownish-gray under skin. Cover with plastic wrap and refrigerate until serving time.

SAUCE:

½ cucumber, peeled   2 T mayonnaise
¼ C sour cream or plain yogurt   1 to 2 tsp onion, grated
2 tsp parsley or chives, finely   1 tsp white vinegar
  chopped   Salt and pepper, to taste

Shred cucumber. Do not drain. Add remaining ingredients and mix well. Chill until serving time.

Microwave: To cook salmon, place in a microwave dish or pie plate. Add 1 teaspoon lemon juice and cover with plastic wrap. Cook on high for 5 to 6 minutes, rotating once, or until fish becomes opaque and flakes. Drain and serve with cucumber sauce.

Hint: This is a very easy but elegant way to serve salmon, especially on a hot day. Poach the salmon early in the day and chill. The sauce, which tastes delicious even made with nonfat yogurt, is very low in fat and calories. It can also be made early in the day or even a day ahead. To serve, place salmon on a lettuce-lined platter and garnish with lemon wedges and a few cherry tomatoes. Sauce may be drizzled over salmon or served on the side.

79

 ALMON LOAF

15 or 16 oz can red or pink salmon	4 slices white bread, crusts
½ C sour cream	removed
1 small onion, diced	1 C milk
½ green pepper, diced	2 eggs, separated
2 T margarine, canola or olive oil	

Drain salmon and discard skin. Bones of salmon are an excellent source of calcium so you may mix them with the salmon in the food processor using the steel blade, otherwise discard them. Sauté onion and pepper in margarine or oil until glossy. Set aside. Soak bread in milk and add to salmon, sautéed onion and pepper, sour cream and egg yolks. Beat egg whites until stiff and fold into salmon mixture. Pour into a greased 9"x5" loaf pan and bake at 350° for 1 hour.

Hint: Yogurt may be substituted for the sour cream. This is a great brunch dish. It's also a good recipe to keep in mind for an emergency supper when you might have little in the house but a can of salmon, a couple of eggs, etc.

 ISH OR SEAFOOD CASSEROLE

2½ lbs scrod, haddock, hake,	1¼ C milk
scallops, shrimp, lobster or	½ lb yellow American cheese,
combination of these	shredded
½ lb mushrooms, sliced	Salt and pepper, to taste
¼ C butter or margarine, divided	4 T dry sherry
2 T flour	½ C bread crumbs

Cook fish in a small amount of water until fish begins to flake, approximately 8 to 10 minutes. Scallops, shrimp or lobster should only be cooked for 2 minutes. Flake fish into large pieces. Sauté mushrooms in 2 tablespoons butter or margarine. In another saucepan, melt 2 tablespoons butter or margarine and whisk in flour until smooth. Add milk gradually, stirring constantly until thickened. Add cheese and continue cooking until cheese melts, stirring to blend well. Add salt and pepper, if desired. Add sherry, mushrooms and fish. Place in a greased casserole and top with bread crumbs. Bake at 300° for 20 minutes.

Hint: This is a low fat version of seafood Newburg, which is laden with egg yolks and cream! In this recipe, you may even substitute low fat American cheese for the regular American cheese. This dish is wonderful for a large crowd or buffet because it can be assembled in advance and then baked right before serving.

SEAFOOD STROGANOFF

1 lb large shrimp, peeled
  and deveined
1 lb sea scallops
½ lb mushrooms, sliced
3 T butter or margarine, divided
2 T dry sherry

2 T flour
⅛ tsp white pepper
1 C chicken bouillon
8 oz sour cream
2 tsp parsley, minced

Rinse seafood and pat dry. Melt 2 tablespoons butter or margarine in a large skillet. Add scallops and shrimp and cook just until scallops are tender, and shrimp have turned pink. Remove from pan. Add the remaining tablespoon of butter or margarine to the skillet and melt. Add mushrooms and sherry and cook just until mushrooms are tender. In a separate bowl, combine bouillon, flour and pepper and add to mushrooms. Cook, stirring constantly until mixture boils. Reduce heat to low and stir in sour cream just until blended. Add scallops and shrimp. Cook over low heat just until hot. Serve over puff pastry shells or rice. Garnish with minced parsley.

Hint: You can substitute lobster for the shrimp. For extra color, add green peas and chopped pimento to the stroganoff, near the end, along with the seafood. This is a perfect dish to serve for the holidays, or a dinner party anytime of the year. Puff pastry shells are found in the frozen food department of most supermarkets. Bake according to the directions on the package.

BAKED SCALLOPS

¾ lb scallops
3 T fresh parsley, chopped
3 T Ritz cracker crumbs
  (4 crackers, crushed)
2 tsp butter or margarine

1 clove garlic, minced
Salt and pepper, to taste
2 T grated Parmesan cheese
  (optional)
Lemon wedges, for garnish

If using large sea scallops, cut them in half. Combine parsley, cracker crumbs and scallops. In an ovenproof casserole, melt butter or margarine and add garlic. Saute for 2 minutes. Add scallop mixture to casserole and mix well. If desired, sprinkle with Parmesan cheese. Bake at 350° for 15 to 20 minutes, or until scallops are done. Garnish with lemon wedges.

Hint: If you use a casserole dish that can be heated on top of the stove you can saute the garlic in the same pan in which you bake the casserole. This saves on the cleanup! This dish can be prepared several hours in advance and baked just before serving.

SAUTEED SEA SCALLOPS

¾ lb sea scallops
¼ C flour
Salt, pepper and paprika, to taste

1 T butter
1 T olive oil
1 T fresh lemon juice

Cut very large scallops in half so that scallops are of uniform size. Season flour with salt, pepper and paprika. Dredge scallops in flour mixture, shaking off excess. Heat butter and olive oil in a frying pan just until hot and bubbling. Add scallops and stir-fry for 3 to 4 minutes. Pour lemon juice into pan and allow to sizzle. Then swirl scallops around in lemon juice. Cook for about 1 more minute. Entire cooking time should not exceed 4 to 5 minutes. Do not overcook the scallops or they will become tough.

Hint: White wine may be substituted for or added to the lemon juice. Sliced mushrooms also may be added before scallops. Heat mushrooms until tender and remove from pan. Add scallops. At the very end, return mushrooms to pan.

SHRIMP DE JONGHE

1½ to 2 lbs shrimp, peeled and deveined
4 to 5 T butter or margarine
¼ tsp paprika
1 clove garlic, minced

¼ C fresh parsley, chopped
Dash cayenne pepper
2 T dry sherry
1 C bread crumbs

Melt butter or margarine in a small saucepan or in a microwave. Add garlic, parsley, paprika, cayenne and sherry. Mix and add bread crumbs. Toss everything together. Place shrimp in a greased 7"x11" baking dish. Top with crumb mixture. Bake at 325° for 25 minutes or until shrimp are pink and crumbs are browned.

Hint: This is a great dish to serve for company because it can be prepared in advance up to the period of baking. Just put it in the oven when you're serving your hors d'oeuvres or salad.

Meat

CHINESE BEEF WITH OYSTER SAUCE

1 lb flank steak, sliced into small
   strips across the grain
2 to 3 T canola or peanut oil
3 cloves garlic, crushed
6 T oyster sauce
½ lb pea pods

¼ tsp salt (optional)
1 C mushrooms, sliced
¼ to ½ tsp sesame oil
½ C chicken broth
½ C cold water
4 tsp cornstarch

Combine chicken broth, cold water and cornstarch and set aside. Preheat canola or peanut oil in wok and add garlic. Stir-fry garlic until it begins to brown. Then remove garlic from wok and discard. Add meat and stir-fry for 2 minutes on high. Add oyster sauce and stir-fry for about 2 minutes more, or until meat is no longer pink. With a slotted spoon, remove meat leaving as much sauce in wok as possible. Add pea pods and sprinkle with salt, if desired. Add mushrooms. Add reserved cornstarch mixture, which has been whisked together, and cook until it thickens. Add sesame oil and cooked meat and heat just until meat is hot. Serve over rice or Chinese noodles.

Hint: Oyster sauce is in the oriental section of most supermarkets. Parboiled broccoli or canned baby corn may be substituted for the pea pods or mushrooms. This is an authentic Chinese dish that almost everyone loves. When stir-fry cooking, feel free to substitute whatever vegetables are in season or that your family enjoys.

CHINESE BEEF WITH PEPPERS AND TOMATOES

1 lb round or flank steak, cut
into strips ¼" to ½" thick
and 1" long
1½ T cornstarch
1 tsp sugar
½ tsp ginger
¼ C soy sauce

3 medium peppers (green, red
or yellow)
1 clove garlic, minced
3 small tomatoes
2 T canola or peanut oil
½ C water

Whisk cornstarch, sugar, ginger and soy sauce until well blended. Pour mixture over meat and mix well. If time permits, refrigerate for at least 30 minutes so that coating will adhere to meat. This may be done up to 24 hours in advance. Cut peppers into thin strips and cut tomatoes into wedges. Quickly brown beef strips a third at a time in hot oil and remove from pan. Reduce heat; add peppers, garlic and water to pan and cook until peppers are tender-crisp, 5 to 6 minutes. Stir in meat and tomatoes and heat through.

Hint: This dish is especially delicious when tomatoes are in season. If you have a garden and are looking for a new way to use your surplus of tomatoes and peppers, try this. Use whatever color peppers you like.

BEEF AND NECTARINE STIR-FRY

1 lb sirloin or flank steak cut
into strips ¼" to ½" thick
and 1" long
1 to 2 T canola or peanut oil
Dash black pepper
3 to 4 T flour
4 T soy sauce

2 T honey
2 red onions, sliced
2 small green peppers, sliced
2 cloves garlic, finely minced
4 nectarines, sliced
Pinch cayenne pepper

Grind pepper over steak pieces. Lightly dredge in flour and then set aside. Combine soy sauce and honey and set aside. Heat oil in wok or frying pan until hot. Stir-fry red onions and green peppers until tender crisp. Add garlic and beef and cook until beef is browned. Add nectarines, reserved soy/honey mixture and cayenne pepper. Stir constantly until nectarines are warm and liquid is reduced to a glaze.

Hint: This may sound like a strange combination but it is a very tasty and colorful dish. It also offers a pleasant contrast of textures; soft nectarines versus crisp peppers and onions. Serve immediately over rice or Chinese noodles.

FAJITAS

1½ lbs flank, sirloin or London Broil or boneless chicken breast

MARINADE:

2 T canola or peanut oil	¼ tsp cumin
½ C soy sauce	Salt, to taste
⅓ C red wine	¼ tsp black pepper
1 tsp onion powder	1 tsp coriander
1 tsp garlic powder	

Combine all ingredients except beef or chicken. Pour over beef or chicken and marinate a minimum of 4 hours or overnight. Grill, broil or pan-fry until cooked to desired doneness. Place on cutting board and cut into strips 3 inches long by ½ inch wide.

ACCOMPANIMENTS:

• Flour tortillas
• Sauteed peppers and onions: Saute 3 to 4 peppers, cut into strips, along with 3 onions, sliced in rounds, in 1 to 2 tablespoons oil. Cook 20 to 25 minutes, stirring occasionally, just until softened. (If extra flavor is desired, add a little marinade liquid to peppers and onions.)
• Guacamole
• Diced tomatoes
• Salsa
• Sour cream

Hint: You may use stir-fry beef or chicken which is available in most supermarkets, and then you won't have to cut up the steak or chicken.

KOREAN STEAK MARINADE

2 to 3 lbs sirloin or flank steak	1 tsp black pepper
1 C soy sauce	5 garlic cloves, minced
2 to 3 T canola oil	2½ T sugar
3 scallions, chopped	

Combine all ingredients except meat. Pour over meat and marinate for at least 2 to 3 hours, or up to 24 hours. Grill or broil until desired degree of doneness is reached.

Hint: You can marinate chicken or turkey cutlets in this sauce and grill them very quickly on each side.

WEET AND SOUR MEATBALLS

2 lbs ground beef	1 C seasoned bread crumbs
½ C cold water	Salt and pepper, to taste

SAUCE:

15 oz can tomato sauce	10 whole peppercorns, tied
4 T lemon juice	in cheesecloth
½ C brown sugar	

Combine ground beef, bread crumbs, water and salt and pepper. Shape into meatballs. Place in a 3 quart saucepan. Combine sauce ingredients and pour over meatballs. Cook over low heat for about 40 to 50 minutes, or until meatballs are cooked.

Hint: Serve over rice for a main course, or in a chafing dish as an hors d'oeuvre. You can substitute ground turkey or chicken for all or part of the ground beef. You don't have to put the peppercorns in cheesecloth, however, you'll have to warn whoever eats the meatballs to "watch out for peppercorns!"

OCK STUFFED CABBAGE

1 small head cabbage, shredded	½ tsp garlic powder
1½ to 2 lbs ground beef,	15 oz tomato sauce
turkey or chicken	8 to 12 oz whole or "crushed
1 egg	berry" cranberry sauce
¾ C bread crumbs	2 T brown sugar

Place shredded cabbage in a Dutch oven. Combine ground beef, egg, bread crumbs and garlic. Shape into meatballs and place on top of cabbage. Combine tomato sauce, cranberry sauce and brown sugar and pour over meatballs. Cover and cook on top of stove or in a 350° oven for one hour. Serve with noodles or rice.

Hint: This tastes almost like stuffed cabbage, but without all the work! To keep this recipe as low in cholesterol as possible, substitute ground chicken or turkey for the beef and use an egg substitute or two egg whites instead of the whole egg. This freezes well.

ITALIAN GROUND BEEF SUB

16 oz loaf Italian bread
1 lb lean ground beef
1 onion, chopped
1 C spaghetti sauce
1 tsp oregano
1 to 1½ C Mozzarella or
    Cheddar cheese, shredded

Cut loaf of bread in half lengthwise. Remove bread from inside of bottom half so that only the shell remains. Saute beef and onion on top of stove until meat is no longer pink. Drain off fat. Add spaghetti sauce and oregano to meat. Place meat mixture in hollowed-out bread and sprinkle with shredded cheese. Cover with top half of bread. Bake at 350° for 15 minutes, or until cheese melts. Let rest for about 5 minutes before slicing. Cut into large slices and serve.

Microwave: Beef may also be cooked in the microwave by placing it in a plastic colander in a deep microwave bowl. (This allows any fat from meat to drain.) Cook on high for 3 to 5 minutes, or until beef is no longer pink. Stir halfway through cooking.

Hint: This has also been called a Superbowl sandwich for it is great to serve while watching the Superbowl or any football game. It's even good when you're not watching TV.

AMERICAN CHOP SUEY

1 lb ground beef
1 T olive or canola oil
16 oz can stewed tomatoes, drained
15 oz can tomato sauce
½ green pepper, diced
1 onion, diced
Salt and pepper, to taste
8 oz elbow macaroni, cooked and
    drained

Saute pepper and onion in oil until tender. Add beef, tomato sauce and tomatoes. Season to taste. Add macaroni and mix well.

Hint: You can substitute ground turkey or chicken for the ground beef.

QUICK TACOS

10 to 12 taco shells
1 lb ground beef

1 pkg taco seasoning mix
¼ C water

Brown beef in skillet. Drain fat. Add taco seasoning mix and water. Bring to a boil. Reduce heat and simmer uncovered, 15 to 20 minutes, stirring occasionally. Place taco shells on cookie sheet. Heat shells in 350° oven 5 to 7 minutes. Fill each shell with 1 to 2 tablespoons cooked meat mixture. Bring tacos to table and let each person top his tacos with the following toppings:

- Shredded lettuce
- Chopped tomato
- Taco sauce or salsa
- Shredded cheese (Monterey Jack, Cheddar or "taco cheese")

Microwave: Place beef in a colander in a deep microwave bowl. Microwave on high 3 to 5 minutes, or until beef is no longer pink. Stir and rotate dish halfway through cooking time. Drain. Stir in seasoning mix and water. Microwave on high 2 more minutes. Microwave taco shells on high 1 minute. Spoon 1 to 2 tablespoons of meat filling into each shell. Serve with toppings listed above.

Hint: This is always a popular dish, especially when children are around. We've served "make your own tacos" several times at my sons' birthday parties or Cub Scout parties and the children always have enjoyed them. Ground turkey or chicken may be substituted for the beef.

EAST-WEST STIR-FRY

1 tsp canola oil
1 lb ground beef or turkey
10¾ oz can chicken broth
1 C carrots, thinly sliced
6 large mushrooms, sliced
½ C scallions, sliced

2 T Worcestershire sauce
1 T soy sauce
1 T cornstarch
10 oz fresh spinach, stems
  removed, torn into pieces

Heat oil in wok or large frying pan. Break ground beef or turkey into chunks and stir-fry 3 minutes or until no longer pink. Remove meat and set aside. Add broth, carrots and mushrooms to wok or pan. Cook over high heat for 3 minutes. Combine Worcestershire sauce, soy sauce and cornstarch and add to pan. Add browned meat and scallions. Bring to a boil; cook 1 minute. Stir in spinach and cook just until wilted.

Hint: This is a quick, nutritious stir-fry dish that uses ground beef or turkey instead of the usual beef strips or cubes. Spinach, carrots and mushrooms are also an unusual vegetable combination. Try using low sodium chicken broth, Worcestershire sauce and soy sauce without sacrificing flavor!

SIRLOIN TIPS DELUXE

1 lb sirloin tips, cut into 2" cubes
3 to 4 T flour
Salt and pepper, to taste
1 T butter or margarine
1 to 2 T olive oil

1 medium onion, diced
1 clove garlic, minced
½ lb fresh mushrooms, sliced
1 T tomato paste
1 C beef broth

Dredge beef in mixture of flour, salt and pepper, shaking off excess. Heat butter or margarine and 1 tablespoon olive oil in a large frying pan. Quickly brown beef, leaving it pink in the center. Remove from pan to a casserole dish. In frying pan, saute onion, garlic and mushrooms, adding 1 tablespoon oil, if necessary. Saute for 7 to 8 minutes, or until onions and mushrooms are tender. Add to meat. Combine tomato paste and broth and place in frying pan. Bring to a boil, while scraping bits from pan, and boil until liquid is reduced by half. Add meat and mushroom mixture to pan and cook briefly, just until meat is hot. Serve as is or make into Stroganoff.

Hint: To make Beef Stroganoff, combine 1 cup sour cream and 2 tablespoons dry sherry and fold into sauce. Either way, this is good served over noodles.

UNGARIAN GOULASH

2 lbs chuck, cubed
1 large onion, diced
2 T canola oil
1 T Hungarian paprika
1½ tsp caraway seeds

1½ to 2 tsp salt
1½ C water
8 oz can tomato sauce
4 to 6 medium potatoes, peeled
 and quartered (optional)

In a Dutch oven, saute onion in oil until slightly browned. Add paprika and stir until dissolved. Add meat and slowly brown on all sides, stirring occasionally. Add the tomato sauce, caraway seeds, salt and water. Cover and simmer for approximately 1½ to 2 hours or until the meat is almost tender. Add potatoes and ½ cup water, if needed. There should be enough liquid to barely cover the potatoes. Add additional salt, if needed. Simmer for 30 minutes longer, or until meat and potatoes are tender.

Hint: This recipe can be made without the potatoes and served over rice or noodles.

LAZED CORNED BEEF

6 to 7 lbs corned beef
6 to 8 whole cloves (optional)
1 C dark brown sugar
1 tsp white vinegar
½ tsp dry mustard
1 T flour

11 oz can mandarin oranges,
 drained
8 oz can crushed pineapple,
 drained
Ginger ale

Put corned beef in large pot and cover with cold water. Boil and then pour water out and cover with cold water again. Boil and reduce to simmer. Cook for 3 to 4 hours or until tender. Drain. Trim off any visible fat. Place corned beef in an ovenproof pan and stud with cloves, if desired. Mix brown sugar, vinegar, mustard and flour and spread over meat. Place mandarin oranges and pineapple on top. Cover bottom of pan with ginger ale. Bake at 350° for 1 hour, basting often. Slice meat and serve.

Hint: This is a wonderful dish to serve for company or at a buffet table because it can be cooked and sliced ahead. The sauce may be reheated and served separately. This works well with any size corned beef. If, for example, you are using a 3 or 4-pound piece of meat, just reduce cooking time until meat is tender. Cut glaze mixture in half and reduce baking time proportionately.

SWEET AND SOUR BRISKET

4 to 5 lbs beef brisket
2 medium onions, peeled and sliced
1 C ketchup
¼ C brown sugar
¼ C fresh lemon juice

½ tsp Worcestershire sauce
½ C water (or more, as needed)
½ C raisins (optional)
6 carrots, peeled and sliced
3 potatoes, peeled and sliced

Sear the meat, fat side down, in a large roasting pan on top of the stove. Turn meat over and sear the other side. Add sliced onions to the pan. Combine ketchup, brown sugar, lemon juice, Worcestershire and water and pour over meat. Cover pan and transfer to oven which has been preheated to 350°. Bake for 3 to 3½ hours, or until meat is tender, checking occasionally to make sure there is enough liquid in the pan. Add more water if necessary. During the last hour, add carrots, potatoes and raisins. When meat is tender, remove from pan and cool. Slice meat and return to pan with gravy from which all the fat has been removed. When ready to serve, heat at 350° in a covered pan.

Hint: This is a delicious one dish meal. It tastes best when made a day in advance.

BELGIAN BRISKET

4 to 5 lbs beef brisket
2 onions, sliced
4 stalks celery, cut into ½" slices
1 C chili sauce

1 tsp salt, or to taste
½ tsp black pepper, or to taste
12 oz beer
¼ C water

Sear meat, fat side down in a large roasting pan on top of stove. Turn meat over and sear other side. Add onions, celery, chili and water to pan. Cover and transfer to preheated 350° oven for 3 hours. Add the beer, cover and cook for another hour, or until meat is tender. Remove meat and cool. Strain gravy and allow to cool until fat can be skimmed off the top. Slice meat and reheat it in skimmed gravy, adding more water if necessary.

Hint: Serve with noodles or over roasted potatoes. This tastes best when made a day in advance.

 UTTERFLIED LEG OF LAMB

5 to 6 lb lamb leg

MARINADE:

1 C red wine

2 cloves garlic, minced

2 bay leaves

½ tsp thyme

¼ C olive oil

1 onion, minced

1 tsp salt

½ tsp oregano

Have butcher debone and butterfly lamb leg. Combine marinade ingredients and mix well. Place lamb in a shallow, nonaluminum pan and top with the marinade. Refrigerate, covering with plastic wrap, and turn occasionally. Marinate for at least 1 to 2 days. Grill for 25 to 30 minutes for medium rare. Do not overcook or meat will be dry.

Hint: This marinade works well for the Butterflied Leg of Lamb and Souvlakia, as well as lamb chops.

 OUVLAKIA

2 lbs lamb, cut into 2" cubes

Cherry tomatoes

Green pepper, cubed

Small onions, quartered

Mushroom caps

Marinade

(see Butterflied Leg of Lamb)

Marinate lamb cubes for 1 to 2 days. Thread on skewers alternately with vegetables. Grill, basting with marinade for 5 to 10 minutes per side, or until they reach desired doneness. Remove lamb and vegetables from skewers and serve on rice pilaf or place in fresh pita bread.

BUTTERFLIED LAMB A LA MOUTARDE

8 oz jar Dijon mustard
½ C olive oil
2 to 3 cloves garlic, minced
1 tsp crushed rosemary
1 tsp thyme

1 tsp bay leaf, crushed
Pepper, to taste
5 to 6 lb leg of lamb, boned and
    butterflied in one piece

Combine all ingredients except lamb. Slash lamb with a knife in several places and spread with marinade mixture on all sides. Cover and marinate for several hours or overnight. Broil lamb in oven broiler or over barbeque grill for 25 to 30 minutes for medium rare, turning several times throughout the cooking. Do not overcook or meat will be dry.

Hint: This is especially delicious when grilled outdoors.

RIGATONI WITH TOMATOES AND SAUSAGES

1 T olive oil	28 oz can Italian plum tomatoes
1½ lb Italian sausages	with tomato puree
(sweet or hot)	Salt and pepper, to taste
3 garlic cloves, finely minced	1 lb rigatoni
3 T parsley, minced	Parmesan cheese, grated

In a frying pan, heat oil over medium-high heat. Fry sausages until well cooked and golden brown. Remove from pan. Cut sausages into 2-inch pieces. Return to frying pan. Add garlic, parsley and tomatoes. Cook over medium-high heat for 10 minutes. Season with salt and pepper, if desired. Meanwhile, cook rigatoni. Drain well. Put pasta on a large platter, making a well in the center. Put sausages in the well and pour sauce over pasta and sausages. Serve with freshly grated Parmesan cheese.

Hint: Turkey sausage may be substituted for pork sausage.

SAUSAGE BAKE

1½ lbs sausage, sliced	4 large potatoes, unpeeled
into 1" chunks	and cut into 2" chunks
2 large green peppers, cubed	2 bay leaves
1 red pepper, cubed	5 cloves garlic, crushed
3 to 4 large onions, cubed	

Place all ingredients into an oiled roasting pan. Bake at 350°, stirring occasionally, for 2 to 2¼ hours, or until sausages and potatoes are golden colored.

Hint: Turkey sausage may be substituted for the pork sausage. This is an easy one dish meal that is great on a fall or winter day when you are home doing projects and want something delicious to eat and smell as it cooks.

HAWAIIAN RIBS

4 to 5 lbs country style pork ribs

SAUCE:

1 C cider vinegar
1 C sugar
1 C orange juice, divided
½ C soy sauce

½ C ketchup
1 medium onion, chopped
3 garlic cloves, minced
3 T cornstarch

Place all sauce ingredients except cornstarch and ¼ cup orange juice in a heavy saucepan. Bring to a boil and then reduce heat and simmer for 10 to 15 minutes. Whisk cornstarch and remaining ¼ cup orange juice together and add to cooked sauce to thicken. Remove sauce from heat. Place some sauce in a roasting pan and cover with ribs. Pour remaining sauce over ribs. Bake at 375° for 1½ to 1¾ hours, turning ribs every ½ hour.

Hint: These ribs are finger-lickin' good! You can bake some potatoes at the same time the ribs are cooking and then use the gravy to put on the potatoes. It's a great combination. Also, chicken parts are delicious baked in this sauce.

PORK CHOPS WITH RAISINS AND ALMONDS

½ tsp salt
4 pork chops, (¾" thick)
⅔ C raw long grain rice
½ C sliced almonds
½ C raisins

2 scallions, minced
½ tsp curry powder
8 oz can tomato sauce
1 C dry white wine

Put salt in heavy frying pan large enough to hold the chops. Brown chops on both sides over moderate heat. Combine the rice, raisins, almonds, scallions and curry powder. Spoon this mixture around the browned chops. Combine the tomato sauce and wine and pour over the chops. Cover the pan and bring the liquid to a boil. Reduce heat and simmer for about 25 to 30 minutes or until the rice and pork chops are tender.

Hint: An electric skillet is handy for making this recipe. A salad and vegetable completes this meal.

PORK CHOPS MARSALA

6 pork chops (¾" to 1" thick) ¼ C marsala wine
1 to 2 T canola oil Dash thyme
10 oz jar guava jelly Dash curry

Brown pork chops in oil on both sides. Pour remaining ingredients over chops. Simmer uncovered, turning often, until tender. Timing depends on thickness of chops, however, as a guide figure approximately 25 to 30 minutes for ¾-inch thick chops.

Hint: If you have never used guava jelly, you might like to try it. The jelly has a delicious and unusual taste that is difficult to describe.

SWEET AND SOUR PORK

1 lb pork sirloin, cut into 1" cubes 1 C canned pineapple chunks,
½ C green pepper, cut into drained
1" cubes ½ C cornstarch
½ C carrot, cut into 1" slices Peanut or canola oil, for
½ C onion, cut into 1" cubes deep-frying

MARINADE:

1½ tsp soy sauce 1 T water
1 tsp cornstarch 1 egg yolk

SWEET AND SOUR SAUCE:

4 T sugar 4 T ketchup
4 T water 3 T cornstarch
4 T vinegar 1 tsp sesame oil

Combine marinade ingredients and pour over meat. Mix well. Allow to marinate for at least ½ hour. Then coat meat with ½ cup cornstarch. Deep-fry in hot oil for 2 minutes. Remove meat and allow oil to reheat. Deep-fry meat again for 1 minute. Remove from oil and set aside. Wipe wok or pan and heat 1 tablespoon oil. Stir-fry vegetables until crisp-tender. Add pineapple and sweet and sour sauce ingredients. Stir mixture until it becomes thick and bubbly. Add fried pork and cook until heated through. Serve over rice.

Hint: Boneless chicken breast may be substituted for the pork.

GRILLED VEAL CHOPS

1 to 1½ lbs veal shoulder or blade chops

MARINADE:

1½ T fresh lemon juice
3 T soy sauce
1 clove garlic, crushed

1 small piece fresh gingerroot, minced, or ½ tsp
powdered ginger

Combine marinade ingredients and mix well. Place veal chops in a shallow nonaluminum pan and pour the mixture over the chops. Marinate for 2 hours or as long as overnight. Place chops on grill and cover. Cook until desired doneness is reached.

Hint: This is a nonfat teriyaki marinade that is also delicious on beef, chicken or fish. Low sodium soy sauce really makes this a healthy marinade. Keep gingerroot fresh for months by placing it in a jar and immersing it in dry sherry. Cover and refrigerate. Any time you need fresh ginger, remove it from jar, peel and chop.

VEAL MARENGO

1½ to 2 lbs veal cubes
1 to 2 T olive oil
1 medium onion, chopped
2 cloves garlic, minced
½ tsp salt, or to taste
⅛ tsp black pepper, or to taste
¼ tsp thyme
Small bay leaf
2 T fresh parsley, minced

2 T flour
½ C chicken broth
½ C dry white wine
1 C canned whole tomatoes,
mashed and drained
6 small (1" to 2") white onions
1 C mushrooms, sliced
Minced parsley, for garnish

Heat oil in a Dutch oven or casserole until hot. Add onion and garlic and saute until golden. Add veal and brown quickly. Add salt, pepper, thyme, bay leaf, minced parsley and flour. Cook, stirring, for 2 minutes. Add broth, wine and tomatoes which have been mashed with a fork. Peel and make cross-cuts (X) in the root ends of the onions and add to the pan. Stir until mixture thickens slightly. Simmer on top of the stove or transfer to the oven and bake at 325° for approximately 1½ to 2 hours or until veal is tender. About 10 minutes before serving add mushrooms. When serving, garnish with extra minced parsley. Serve over noodles or rice.

Hint: This dish may be prepared on top of the stove or baked in the oven for about the same length of time. It is easy to serve for guests because it can be prepared in advance and kept in the oven until you are ready to use it.

EAL PICCATA

1 lb veal cutlets
2 to 3 T flour
½ tsp paprika
¼ tsp black pepper
2 T olive oil

⅓ C white wine
⅓ C chicken broth
Juice of half to one lemon
Lemon slices, for garnish

Pound veal cutlets wafer thin. Dust each piece with flour seasoned with paprika and black pepper. Brown in olive oil; remove to a platter. Add wine, chicken broth and lemon juice to skillet. Return veal cutlets to skillet and simmer until sauce thickens. Garnish with lemon slices.

Hint: Chicken or turkey cutlets may be substituted for the veal.

Poultry

CHINESE-STYLE ROAST CHICKEN

5 lb roasting chicken or	3 T dry sherry
4 to 5 lbs chicken parts	1 tsp ground ginger
½ C hoisin sauce	½ tsp dry mustard
¼ C soy sauce	2 scallions, chopped
1 T brown sugar	

Combine everything except chicken and scallions. Pour mixture over chicken and marinate in the refrigerator for 2 to 4 hours, turning frequently. After marinating, drain chicken and reserve marinade. Roast whole chicken at 350° for 1½ hours (1 hour if using parts). To serve, heat reserved marinade in a saucepan and pour over chicken. Garnish with chopped scallions.

Hint: Hoisin sauce is in the oriental section of most supermarkets. This marinade makes a tasty gravy. Bake potatoes or rice in the oven while the chicken is cooking and serve with the gravy.

ROASTED HERB CHICKEN

4 to 5 lb roasting chicken	1 tsp rosemary
2 T olive oil	Black pepper, to taste
2 cloves garlic, crushed	

Wash chicken and dry well with paper towels. Combine ingredients and rub over entire surface of chicken. Marinate for several hours or overnight. Place on a rack in a roasting pan and cover with foil. Bake at 500° for 45 minutes. Then remove foil and baste with pan juices. Continue baking for 15 to 20 more minutes, or until juices run clear.

Hint: You can marinate this chicken in the morning before you go to work and pop it in the oven as soon as you get home. By the time you've made a salad and vegetables and gone through the mail, the chicken will be ready!

CHICKEN MARSALA

1 lb boneless chicken breasts
2 to 3 T flour
Salt and pepper, to taste
1 T dried (3 T fresh) oregano
2 to 3 T olive oil
½ lb mushrooms, sliced
⅓ to ½ C marsala wine

Pound chicken breasts lightly. Dredge in mixture of flour, salt, pepper and oregano. Heat oil in large skillet and saute chicken on both sides until lightly browned. Add mushrooms and wine. Cover and cook 5 to 10 minutes or until chicken is tender.

Hint: This is an elegant but easy low fat entree. Veal or turkey cutlets may be substituted for the chicken.

CHICKEN FLORENTINE

2 whole chicken breasts, boned and halved
⅓ C flour
½ tsp salt, or to taste
1 egg, beaten
1 to 2 T olive oil
10 oz pkg frozen chopped spinach
2 T Parmesan cheese, grated
2 oz Mozzarella or Swiss cheese, sliced
⅓ C white wine
Juice of ½ lemon
½ C chicken broth

Pound chicken breasts to uniform thickness. Dredge chicken in flour mixed with salt. Dip in beaten egg. Heat oil in a frying pan and sauté chicken 6 minutes on each side. While chicken is cooking, cook spinach according to package directions; drain and set aside. Remove chicken from frying pan and place in a greased ovenproof dish. Cover with spinach. Sprinkle Parmesan cheese over spinach. Cover with sliced Mozzarella or Swiss cheese. Bake at 350° for 10 to 15 minutes, or until chicken is tender and cheese is melted. While chicken is baking, make sauce by adding wine and lemon juice to frying pan. Simmer and scrape up bits in pan, until liquid is reduced to half. Add chicken broth, stir and simmer 2 more minutes. Pour over chicken or serve separately.

Hint: This is a colorful and tasty dish that can be prepared in advance to the point of placing the chicken in the oven. Just before serving, bake chicken and make sauce as instructed above. Glazed Carrots (pg. 118) and Barley and Mushroom Pilaf (pg. 134) or Rice Pilaf (pg. 137) go well with this.

MICROWAVE CHEEZY CRUMB CHICKEN

4 boneless chicken breast halves (approx.1 lb)

2 T butter or margarine, melted

1 to 1½ C cheese crackers, crushed

Dip chicken in melted butter or margarine. Roll in cracker crumbs. Arrange pieces on a flat microwave baking dish or on a dinner plate. Cover with a piece of paper towel. Microwave on high 5 to 6 minutes, turning halfway through. Let stand, covered, for 1 to 2 minutes before serving.

Hint: One pound fish fillets, such as sole or flounder, may be substituted for the chicken; however, reduce the cooking time to approximately 4 minutes. Using paper towels as a covering for the chicken or fish enables the crumbs to become somewhat crispy. In fact, whenever you want a crispy coating for food cooked in the microwave, use paper towels rather than plastic wrap or wax paper.

GRILLED LEMON MUSTARD CHICKEN

2 lbs boneless chicken breasts, halved

¼ C fresh herbs such as basil, parsley, oregano or rosemary, chopped

¼ C Dijon mustard

½ C fresh lemon juice

Rind of one lemon, chopped

¼ tsp black pepper

In a small bowl combine all ingredients, except chicken, to make the marinade. Place chicken in a nonaluminum pan and pour marinade over it. Marinate for 2 to 4 hours in the refrigerator. Grease grids of grill with oil or spray with nonstick spray. Grill chicken for 6 to 9 minutes per side, or until cooked through. Check carefully for doneness so that the chicken will not get overcooked and dry.

Hint: This is a wonderful fat free marinade that has an intense lemon flavor. If not overcooked, it tastes very moist and juicy.

CHICKEN BREASTS IN FILO

¼ lb butter (use for sauteing)
1 onion, finely chopped
½ lb mushrooms, finely chopped
2 T parsley, minced
1 clove garlic, minced
1½ T flour
⅓ C vermouth

Salt and pepper, to taste
2 T olive oil
4 boneless chicken breasts, halved
16 sheets filo dough
⅓ C melted butter (to brush
  on filo)
Bread crumbs

In a skillet, heat 3 tablespoons butter and saute onion until golden. Set aside. Heat 3 more tablespoons butter and saute mushrooms until juices evaporate, then add onions, parsley and garlic and saute a little more. Stir in flour, mixing well and add vermouth. Stir over medium heat until thickened. Season with salt and pepper. Set aside. In skillet, heat remaining butter and oil and saute breasts 1 minute on each side. Wrap one breast in filo at a time, keeping unused sheets between damp dish towels. Brush butter on one sheet of filo. Sprinkle on bread crumbs, cover with another sheet of filo and butter again. Place chicken on filo and put a quarter of the mushroom mixture on top and fold it like an envelope, tucking in corners. Brush butter over the top and bake at 350° for 35 minutes or until golden.

Yield: 8 chicken filo packets

Hint: Filo dough is paper thin and is used often in Middle Eastern cooking. When baked it results in a very flaky dough. It is found in the freezer section of most supermarkets. Remove it from the freezer and place in the refrigerator several hours or the day before you intend to use it. Once the package of filo is opened, the dough will dry out quickly unless it is covered by a damp cloth. The dough is very delicate so it is wise to use a goosefeather brush or soft paint brush to brush the butter on the dough. When using filo, use butter rather than margarine.

FINGER LICKIN' CHICKEN WINGS

2 lbs chicken wings
½ tsp garlic powder
½ C honey

½ C soy sauce
½ C ketchup

Remove outer tips from wings and discard. Sprinkle wings with garlic powder and bake at 375° for 15 minutes. Combine honey, soy sauce and ketchup. Pour over wings and bake for 45 to 60 minutes longer.

Hint: These wings are finger lickin' good. Try them and you'll see how they got their name!

STIR-FRY CHICKEN WITH APPLES

2 Golden Delicious or Granny
  Smith apples
1 to 2 T canola or peanut oil
1 lb boneless chicken breast,
  cut into ¼" to ½" thick
  and 1" long slices
2 medium red or white onions, sliced
1 medium green pepper, sliced

1 medium red pepper, sliced
1 C celery, diagonally sliced
2 T cornstarch
6 T apple juice or cider
¼ tsp salt (optional)
Dash pepper
3 T soy sauce
3 T cider vinegar

Core and slice apples. Heat 1 to 1½ tablespoons oil in wok or non-stick skillet. Stir-fry chicken until cooked; remove it from the pan. Add peppers, onion and celery; stir-fry in remaining oil until crisp-tender. Return chicken to the pan containing vegetables. Add apples; stir-fry until they are hot. Combine remaining ingredients and add to chicken mixture. Cook until the sauce thickens.

Hint: This is an attractive dish with an unusual combination of tastes and colors. Yellow and green apples, red and green peppers and red and white onions, give the dish its interesting color and texture. Also, this is very nutritious because it is low in fat and high in fiber. It is tasty served over white or brown rice or fresh Chinese noodles. Low sodium soy sauce may be substituted for traditional soy sauce.

CRANBERRIED CHICKEN

6 chicken breasts, split
4 T soy sauce
4 T fresh lemon juice
½ tsp garlic powder

3 T margarine
1 lb can whole cranberry sauce
  or homemade sauce

Combine all ingredients, except chicken, in a saucepan and bring to a boil. Place chicken in a baking pan, skin side down. Cover with sauce and bake at 425° for 30 minutes. Turn chicken, reduce oven to 350°, and bake for 30 minutes more, basting about four times.

Hint: This recipe is especially nice to serve during the cranberry season. Use low sodium soy sauce, if desired. If you want to reduce fat, remove the skin before cooking.

103

CHICKEN WITH HOISIN SAUCE

1 lb boneless chicken breasts
cut into 1" cubes
1 T soy sauce
1 T sugar
1 T cornstarch
½ can water chestnuts, sliced
2 T hoisin sauce

1 C mushrooms, sliced
¼ lb pea pods
1 red or green pepper, cut
into 1" cubes
½ C cashews, salt rinsed off
2 to 3 T peanut or canola oil

Combine soy sauce, sugar and cornstarch and marinate chicken cubes in this mixture for at least ½ hour in the refrigerator. Heat wok and add 1 to 2 tablespoons oil. Stir-fry chicken until it turns white. Remove. Add 1 tablespoon oil to hot wok. Stir-fry vegetables until slightly cooked (still crisp). Add reserved chicken, cashews and hoisin sauce. Stir until heated through. Serve with white rice or fried rice.

Hint: This is one of the easiest and most delicious stir-fry dishes. You can substitute peanuts for the cashews. Organization is the key to preparing any stir-fry dish. Everything should be cut up before you begin cooking. You can do this several hours in advance. The chicken may be marinated for several hours or overnight. Once the wok is hot, toss everything together, as directed. Also, if you don't have a wok, an electric frying pan or Dutch oven will work well for stir-frying. The reason a wok is so beneficial is because you only need a small amount of oil to cook in it. The sloping sides allow the same small amount of oil to be tossed around, whereas a flat bottomed vessel seems to "eat up the oil" and you constantly have to add more to it.

CURRIED HONEY CHICKEN

3 to 4 lbs chicken, cut into
quarters or eighths
2 T margarine
½ C honey

¼ C prepared mustard
Salt, to taste
1 to 2 tsp curry powder
½ C almonds, toasted and chopped

Wash and dry chicken. Melt margarine and whisk in remaining ingredients. Roll chicken pieces in mixture to coat both sides. Arrange chicken, meaty side up, in a single layer in the baking pan. Bake at 375° for 1 hour, basting occasionally, until chicken is tender and richly glazed.

Hint: This is one of my family's favorite chicken dishes. Leftovers, served hot or cold, are delicious. To toast almonds, bake at 350° for 3 to 4 minutes.

Moo Goo Gai Pan

1 lb boneless chicken breast, sliced	3 C bok choy, diagonally sliced
2 T soy sauce ⎱ coating	1 C celery, diagonally sliced
1 T cornstarch ⎰	1 C mushrooms, sliced
2 T peanut or canola oil, divided	½ to 1 tsp sesame oil
¼ lb pea pods	

GRAVY MIXTURE:

1 C chicken broth	1½ T cornstarch

Combine chicken and coating. Preheat wok and add 1 tablespoon oil. Add coated chicken and stir-fry for 5 to 7 minutes or until meat is cooked. Remove to serving bowl and add 1 tablespoon more oil to wok. Heat oil and add celery and bok choy. Stir-fry for 3 minutes; then add mushrooms and pea pods and stir-fry for 2 more minutes. Add gravy mixture, reserved chicken and sesame oil. Serve over hot rice or fresh Chinese noodles.

Hint: Why not use the same bowl for preparation as serving? You save in the cleanup. Spaghetti may be substituted for the fresh noodles and shrimp may be substituted for the chicken.

Oven-Fried Chicken

2½ to 3 lb chicken, cut into	1 to 1½ C nonfat or low
quarters or eighths	fat plain yogurt or
1½ to 2 C oat flakes, corn	1 to 2 egg whites, beaten
flakes or bran flakes	½ to 1 tsp garlic powder,
	or to taste

Crush cereal flakes by hand (in plastic bag) so that flakes are just coarsely chopped. Add garlic powder and any other seasonings of your choice to cereal. Dip chicken pieces into yogurt or egg whites and then into seasoned cereal. Place on a foil-lined cookie sheet or broiler rack that you sprayed with cooking spray. Bake at 375° for 50 to 60 minutes or until chicken is crispy on the outside and cooked through on the inside.

Hint: To reduce the fat remove the skin from the chicken before coating with yogurt. The yogurt keeps the chicken moist on the inside, while the outside becomes crispy, even without the skin. If you use nonfat yogurt, or egg whites, this dish will be very low in fat. Fish fillets such as scrod or haddock may be prepared in the same manner. When preparing fish, however, bake at 450° for 10 minutes per inch of thickness.

CHICKEN DIJONNAISE

2½ to 3 lb chicken, quartered or cut into eighths
⅓ C Dijon mustard or mixture of Dijon coarse grained and Pommery mustard
Black pepper, to taste
⅓ C dry white wine or vermouth
½ C plain yogurt

Coat chicken with mustards and marinate for at least 2 to 3 hours in an ovenproof baking pan. Just before cooking, season chicken with pepper and pour wine or vermouth around it. Bake at 375° for 45 to 55 minutes, or until chicken is completely cooked. Scrape the mustard off the chicken pieces into the baking dish. Remove the chicken and place it on a serving platter. Cover with foil to keep warm. Skim off any fat from the cooking juices and set the baking dish over medium heat. Bring to a boil and whisk in the yogurt. Simmer until sauce is slightly reduced and spoon over chicken.

Hint: This low fat chicken dish is an adaptation of a traditional chicken dijonnaise recipe that uses cream. The yogurt gives it a delicious flavor that is much lower in fat, cholesterol and calories. Serve it with Oven French Fries (pg. 130) or baked potatoes which bake at the same time.

CHICKEN CACCIATORE

1 T olive oil
2½ to 3 lbs chicken, quartered
2 onions, sliced
3 cloves garlic, minced
14½ oz can diced tomatoes
Black pepper, to taste
2 small zucchini, sliced
1 tsp oregano
½ tsp basil
1 small green pepper, cubed
2 C mushrooms, sliced
½ C dry white wine or vermouth

Saute garlic and onion in oil until soft, not brown. Add chicken pieces which have had as much visible fat removed as possible. Slowly cook on both sides until golden. Add all remaining ingredients and cover pan. Turn chicken over periodically and baste with pan juices and vegetables. Cook for approximately 40 to 45 minutes or until chicken is completely cooked.

Hint: This is very low in fat and calories and has a delicious flavor. You can adjust the seasonings and amounts of vegetables to suit your taste. Serve over rice, noodles or with baked potatoes.

106

ℬAKED CHICKEN ORIENTAL

2½ to 3 lb chicken, cut into quarters or eighths
11 oz can mandarin oranges, drained
4 scallions, finely chopped
2 cloves garlic, finely chopped
1 tsp fresh gingerroot, finely chopped or grated
2 T soy sauce
1 tsp sesame oil
1 C orange marmalade

Make marinade by mixing everything together except chicken and mandarin oranges. Coat chicken with marinade and refrigerate for at least 2 hours. Bake at 375° for 1 hour, basting occasionally. Add mandarin oranges during last few minutes of baking and then carefully remove from sauce to use as garnish for chicken.

Hint: This is one of the all time favorite chicken recipes from my cooking classes. It is low in fat and cholesterol and is great served with Chinese Fried Rice (pg. 136) or Lo Mein (pg. 135). Even plain rice or noodles are okay because the chicken makes a delicious gravy for them.

ℴRANGE ALMOND CHICKEN BREASTS

1 C bread crumbs
¼ C almonds, finely chopped
½ tsp salt, or to taste
⅛ tsp pepper
2 T fresh parsley, chopped
¼ C frozen orange juice concentrate, thawed and undiluted
1 T margarine, melted
3 chicken breasts, split

Combine bread crumbs, almonds, salt, pepper and parsley. Mix well. Combine orange juice concentrate and margarine. Dip chicken breasts into this mixture. Then dip into crumb mixture. Bake at 350° for 55 to 60 minutes.

Hint: You can assemble these chicken breasts in advance and bake them when needed. They are also delicious served cold and are great for a picnic!

SKILLET CHERRY CHICKEN

12 oz jar cherry preserves
2 T lemon juice
4 whole cloves
¼ tsp salt
¼ tsp allspice
¼ tsp mace

½ C flour
1 tsp salt, or to taste
2½ to 3 lbs chicken, cut into
   quarters or eighths
2 to 3 T olive or canola oil

Combine first six ingredients and set aside. Combine flour and salt in plastic bag. Add chicken pieces, shaking to coat. Brown chicken in oil in skillet over medium heat, turning with tongs. Cover and cook for 15 minutes. Drain off fat. Add cherry mixture and cover. Simmer over low heat, skin side up for 15 minutes. Turn and simmer 15 more minutes or until chicken is tender.

Hint: As the chicken cooks, a delicious gravy is formed. Serve over rice.

PARMESAN CHICKEN

2½ to 3 lb chicken, cut into
   quarters or eighths
1 C bread crumbs
½ C Parmesan cheese, grated
½ tsp garlic powder

½ tsp paprika
¼ tsp pepper
2 T parsley, chopped
4 T margarine, melted

Combine all ingredients except chicken and margarine. Dip chicken into margarine and then into crumb mixture. Bake on a foil-lined cookie sheet at 350° for 1 hour.

Hint: To reduce fat and calories, you may substitute an egg white for the melted margarine. The crumbs will adhere to the chicken just as well. This is delicious served hot or cold.

FANCY CHICKEN

2½ to 3 lbs chicken, cut into
   quarters or eighths

1 C orange marmalade
3 to 4 T ketchup

Combine marmalade and ketchup. Spread on skin side of chicken. Bake at 400° for 20 minutes. Reduce heat to 350° and bake for 15 minutes. Turn and bake for 30 more minutes, basting occasionally.

Hint: Who ever heard of "fancy chicken" that's so easy to make?

CHICKEN TERIYAKI

3 to 4 lbs chicken, cut into
quarters or eighths
⅔ C soy sauce
½ C dry white wine or vermouth
½ C sugar

¼ tsp powdered ginger or
1 tsp fresh ginger, minced
2 cloves garlic, minced
1 T canola or peanut oil

Combine everything except chicken and then marinate chicken in mixture for several hours or overnight. Drain chicken from marinade and bake at 350° for 1 hour, basting occasionally with reserved marinade. Broil for the last few minutes so that chicken gets slightly glazed.

Hint: Remove the skin from the chicken before cooking it to keep this low in fat. In fact, the oil may be omitted from the marinade without affecting the taste. This marinade may also be used for beef. Both the chicken or beef teriyaki are delicious on the grill.

CORNISH HENS WITH APRICOT SAUCE

4 Cornish hens
1 small onion, finely diced
10 to 12 oz jar apricot jam

½ C ketchup
1 orange, quartered

Beat jam with a fork until smooth. Add ketchup and onion. Place an orange quarter inside each hen. Place hens in a large roasting pan and brush with jam mixture. Cover with foil and bake at 325° for 45 minutes. Uncover and raise oven temperature to 350°. Bake for an additional 15 to 30 minutes, basting often, until hens are golden. Allow hens to sit for 5 to 10 minutes before cutting in half. Remove orange from hen.

Hint: Serve each person a half or whole hen, depending on his or her appetite and what else is being served with the meal. The orange gives the hen a nice flavor. This recipe may also be used for chicken. Orange Rice (pg. 138) would make a delicious stuffing for the hens. If you use the rice, eliminate the orange quarters from this recipe. Many of the recipes for chicken parts in this book may be used for Cornish hens.

109

Roast Turkey

Roasting times for turkey are based on a preheated 325° oven. Plan enough time to allow the bird to stand for about 20 minutes before carving. This makes the meat juicier and easier to carve. A stuffed 8 to 12-pound turkey roasts for about 3½ to 4½ hours. It is best to use a meat thermometer to make certain turkey is cooked properly. Insert it into the thickest part of thigh, not touching bone. (If a turkey has a pop-up thermometer, when cooked, the thermometer pops up.) Make a foil tent by tearing off a piece of heavy duty foil 5 to 10 inches longer than the turkey. Turn foil to cover turkey from side to side. Crimp foil onto long sides of pan to hold into place. Roast according to the time chart on the turkey label. To achieve a golden brown color, carefully remove foil during last 30 to 35 minutes before roasting is finished. Baste a few times with pan juices and cook until meat thermometer reads 180 to 185°.

Hint: I learned this simple and delicious recipe from my mother. The turkey always comes out juicy and has a beautiful golden color.

Turkey Stuffing Technique

Turkeys should only be stuffed at the last minute. However, stuffing may be prepared several hours in advance or the night before. The cavity of the turkey should be stuffed loosely because the stuffing expands as it cooks. Allow ½ to ¾ cup stuffing per pound of turkey. If you are pressed for time, an unstuffed turkey cooks faster than a stuffed one. Also, if you prefer to bake the stuffing separately, spoon it into a greased dish. Dot top with butter or margarine and sprinkle with a little stock. Cover. Bake at 325° for 1 hour, uncovering during last 15 minutes. To keep the stuffing in the turkey, you need to close the neck and body cavities. Fold the neck skin over the back and fasten with a skewer, trussing pins, clean string, or toothpicks; twist the wingtips under the back of the turkey to rest against the neck skin. To close the body cavity, use skewers, or tuck ends of legs under a band of skin at the tail, or into metal hock-locks, if provided, or tie legs together with clean string.

Hint: Unwaxed and unflavored dental floss may be used if you don't have any string. After turkey is cooked, remove all the stuffing. Serve turkey and stuffing within 2 hours. If not used within this time, make sure to refrigerate turkey and stuffing separately so that bacteria that can cause food poisoning does not have a chance to grow.

TRADITIONAL BREAD STUFFING FOR TURKEY

(for a 10 to 12-pound bird)

2 qts bread cubes (12 slices white
  bread, toasted and cut into cubes)
2 medium onions, diced
3 celery stalks, diced
2 medium apples, chopped
6 T butter or margarine
Salt and pepper, to taste
¼ C fresh parsley, chopped

2 tsp fresh thyme, minced or
  ¾ tsp dried and crumbled
2 tsp fresh sage or ¾ tsp
  dried, and crumbled
1 egg, beaten
½ to 1 C stock (from giblets,
  see Turkey Stock below) or
  bouillon, as needed, to moisten

Toast bread in a toaster or bake at 275° until crisp and dry, turning often, about 30 minutes total. Let cool and cut toast into cubes. Transfer to a large, deep bowl (can be done one day in advance). Melt butter or margarine in a large frying pan over medium heat. Add celery and onions. Cook until onions are soft but not brown, stirring occasionally. Add herbs and salt and pepper. Remove from heat. Pour over bread cubes and toss gently. Add apples, egg and enough stock until just barely moist.

TURKEY STOCK:

Turkey neck, heart, outer wing
  tips and gizzard
1 carrot, cut in chunks
1 stalk celery, cut in chunks

1 small onion, cut in chunks
1 bay leaf
Water

Place all ingredients in a pot and add enough water to cover. Cook for 1 hour or until tender. Strain and use as needed. If desired, chop gizzards and add to stuffing or gravy.

Hint: This is my family's traditional stuffing recipe. As a child, I watched my grandmother and mother make this every Thanksgiving. In fact, when I make it, I use my grandmother's stuffing bowl.

TURKEY CUTLETS WITH BALSAMIC VINEGAR

¾ lb boneless turkey cutlets,
each ¼" thick
¼ C balsamic vinegar
2 tsp honey
½ C bread crumbs

Salt and pepper, to taste
2 to 3 T olive oil
2 cloves garlic, minced
¼ C dry white wine or vermouth
Minced parsley, for garnish

Mix vinegar and honey until honey dissolves. Set aside. Season bread crumbs with salt and pepper. Dredge turkey in crumbs, pressing well to make them adhere. Heat 1 to 2 tablespoons oil in a large skillet until it is hot. Saute the turkey cutlets for 1 minute per side. Transfer them to a platter. Add the remaining oil and garlic to the pan and cook just until garlic is golden. Add the white wine or vermouth. Boil the mixture until sauce is reduced to 2 tablespoons. Add reserved honey and vinegar mixture and boil until it is syrupy. Put the cutlets back in the pan and simmer for 3 to 4 more minutes or until they are completely cooked. Garnish with parsley.

Hint: The combination of the balsamic vinegar and wine give this a delicate and almost fruity flavor. Thinly pounded chicken breasts may be substituted for the turkey cutlets.

STIR-FRY TURKEY AND VEGETABLES

1 lb turkey cutlets, cut into
1" cubes
3 T soy sauce
¼ tsp garlic powder
2 T canola or peanut oil
1 green pepper, cubed

1 red pepper, cubed
4 oz mushrooms, sliced
4 scallions, sliced
1 T cornstarch
½ C chicken broth

Marinate turkey in soy sauce and garlic powder. Heat oil in wok or skillet over medium-high heat. Stir-fry turkey for 3 minutes, or until no longer pink. Add peppers and stir-fry one minute. Add mushrooms and scallions; stir-fry 1 more minute. Combine cornstarch and broth and mix well. Add to wok. Stir until thickened.

Hint: Boneless chicken breast may be substituted for the turkey.

TURKEY AND ARTICHOKE SCALLOPINI

2 T Parmesan cheese, grated
2 T flour
½ tsp oregano
1 lb turkey breast cutlets
2 T olive oil
4 oz fresh mushrooms, sliced
4 scallions, sliced

9 oz pkg frozen (or 14 oz can)
   artichoke hearts, drained
   and cut in half
⅓ C chicken broth
2 T white wine
2 T fresh lemon juice

Combine Parmesan cheese, flour and oregano. Coat turkey cutlets with this mixture. Heat 1 tablespoon oil in nonstick skillet until hot. Cook turkey until it is no longer pink, about 2 minutes on each side. Remove to warm platter; keep warm. Heat 1 more tablespoon of oil in skillet and add mushrooms and scallions. Cook until soft. Add artichoke hearts. Stir in remaining ingredients and bring to a boil. Pour over turkey cutlets.

Hint: Boneless chicken breasts may be substituted for the turkey, however the chicken breasts must be pounded until they are quite thin and flat. This dish is very tasty served over angel hair pasta.

113

Vegetables and Potatoes

ALMOND ASPARAGUS

1 lb asparagus
2 T butter or margarine
1 T fresh lemon juice
1 tsp lemon rind, grated
½ C slivered almonds
Salt and pepper, to taste

Peel asparagus if at all woody. Cut off bottoms and cut remaining stalks into diagonal pieces. Saute in large pan with butter or margarine, salt, pepper and lemon rind. Asparagus may also be microwaved. Drizzle with lemon juice. Cover pan and cook for 3 to 4 minutes or until tender. Sprinkle with almonds.

Microwave: To cook 1 pound peeled and cut asparagus, place in a covered dish with ¼ cup water. Cook on high for 5 to 7 minutes, or until tender.

Hint: The fresh lemon juice and rind really emphasize the unique flavor of asparagus.

CRUMB TOPPING FOR VEGETABLES

1½ to 2 T butter or margarine
¼ C bread crumbs
1 T fresh lemon juice

Melt butter or margarine in a small saucepan over medium heat. Add bread crumbs and mix well. Add lemon juice and mix until mixture begins to turn golden. Watch carefully or mixture will burn. Sprinkle mixture over 1 to 1½ pounds cooked fresh green beans, broccoli, cauliflower or asparagus.

Hint: This is one of the easiest and most versatile ways to dress up vegetables. I recall watching my grandmother make this for special dinners. You can make this a few hours in advance, leave it on the stove until the vegetables are cooked, then reheat it briefly before sprinkling over the cooked vegetables.

GRATED ZUCCHINI

1 T butter or margarine
1 T olive or canola oil
2 cloves garlic, minced

3 unpeeled zucchini, grated
Salt, pepper and fresh nutmeg,
to taste

Melt butter or margarine and oil in a frying pan or wok. Add garlic and sauté for 2 to 3 minutes. Add zucchini and toss or stir for 5 to 6 minutes. Season with salt, pepper and nutmeg.

Hint: Most of us are accustomed to only having zucchini sliced. When grated, it takes on a totally different taste and texture. It's really good. The food processor makes grating the zucchini a cinch. You don't have to use fresh nutmeg, however it has a nicer taste and aroma. To get fresh nutmeg, buy a whole nutmeg (about the size of a marble) and use a small tin grater to shave or grate as much as you need. Whole nutmeg is found in the spice section of supermarkets or health food stores.

STIR-FRY ZUCCHINI

1 large onion, thinly sliced
2 cloves garlic, crushed
¼ C brown sugar
1 lb zucchini, thinly sliced

1 to 2 T canola or peanut oil
1 T water
3 T soy sauce

Stir-fry onion and garlic in oil for 1 minute. Add zucchini and brown sugar. Stir-fry for about 5 minutes. Add water and soy sauce and cook about 5 minutes more or just until zucchini is tender.

Hint: This is a quick and tasty way to cook zucchini, a vegetable which is readily available year round. Low sodium soy sauce can be used.

PICKLED GARDEN MEDLEY

2¾ C cold water
1 C white vinegar
⅓ to ½ C sugar
2 T salt
1½ tsp pickling spices
2 garlic cloves, crushed
4 to 5 fresh dill sprigs, or to taste

5 C fresh raw vegetables such as: broccoli flowerets; cauliflower flowerets; carrot slices or sticks; zucchini slices; celery slices; red or green pepper slices; green tomatoes, quartered; pea pods, etc.

Combine everything except vegetables to form pickling brine. Add vegetables and place in a large glass jar or bowl and cover. Refrigerate at least 24 to 36 hours before serving. Vegetables remain crisp, bright colored and delicious for up to 6 or 7 days.

Hint: These vegetables are wonderful to keep in the refrigerator for a tasty nonfat snack. They are also great for picnics, barbecues and parties. The best features of this recipe are that the vegetables don't have to be cooked, they contain no fat, and they can be prepared a few days prior to serving. A jar of this medley makes a wonderful gift any time of the year, especially for someone who is on a low fat diet. You can find pickling spices, a packaged blend of spices, in the spice section of the supermarket.

FREEZER PICKLES

2 qts cucumbers, unpeeled and thinly sliced
1 C white vinegar

2 T salt
2 onions, thinly sliced
1½ C sugar

Slice and mix cucumbers and onions. Let stand in colander for 2 to 3 hours and drain. Combine remaining ingredients, stirring until mixture becomes thin. Transfer cucumbers and onions to a large container and pour mixture over them. Freeze in jars or plastic containers.

Hint: These pickles are great to make during summer when cucumbers are abundant. They are much easier to make than traditional pickles that need to be processed and canned. They will keep in the freezer for months and make nice gifts, especially if packed in pretty jelly jars or any attractive jar that you have recycled.

CAULIFLOWER WITH A TANG

1 head cauliflower
½ C mayonnaise
2 tsp Dijon mustard

1 to 2 T chives, minced (optional)
¾ C Cheddar or Swiss cheese, grated

Cook cauliflower on top of the stove or in the microwave just until almost tender; it should still be slightly crisp. Drain and place in a pie plate or similar size overproof pan. Combine mayonnaise, mustard and chives and spread over cauliflower. Sprinkle with grated cheese. Bake at 375° for 15 to 20 minutes or until cheese melts.

Microwave: To cook a 6 to 7-inch cauliflower (approximately 1½ to 2 pounds) place in a pie plate with 2 tablespoons water. Cover with plastic wrap and cook on high for 8 to 11 minutes.

Hint: You may substitute two 10-ounce packages of frozen cauliflower for the fresh cauliflower. If you have fresh chives, this is especially tasty. It is a good dish to serve guests because it may be completely prepared ahead and just popped into the oven for the last 15 to 20 minutes.

GLAZED CARROTS

1 lb carrots
2 to 3 T butter or margarine
2 to 3 T brown sugar

½ tsp paprika
Salt, to taste

Peel and slice carrots. Steam or microwave until just barely tender. Drain well. In a large frying pan, melt butter or margarine. Add carrots and sprinkle with brown sugar, paprika and salt. Cook over medium heat, stirring occasionally, until glazed.

Microwave: To cook 1 pound peeled, trimmed and sliced carrots, place in a covered dish with 2 tablespoons water. Cook on high for 4 to 6 minutes.

Hint: This is a great dish to master because it is delicious, colorful, goes well with most everything and is easy to make and serve. Also, carrots are usually inexpensive and are available all year.

MARINATED CARROT STICKS

1 lb carrot sticks
4 T olive or canola oil
1 tsp pickling spices

⅓ C cider vinegar
2 small cloves garlic, crushed
½ tsp salt

Peel carrots and cut into narrow strips. Cover with marinade and refrigerate. Drain and serve.

Hint: This tastes best when made at least a day before serving. You can find pickling spices, a packaged blend of spices, in the spice section of the supermarket.

STEAMED BRUSSELS SPROUTS AND BABY CARROTS

1 lb brussels sprouts
12 to 16 oz baby carrots
2 to 3 T butter or margarine

1½ to 2 T grainy Dijon mustard
Salt and black pepper, to taste
2 T parsley, chopped

Trim the ends of the brussels sprouts and score an X into each end to ensure even cooking. Remove any tough outer leaves and wash carefully under cold running water. Peel and place the carrots in a vegetable steamer and steam over medium heat for 8 to 10 minutes or until they are just beginning to get tender. Add the brussels sprouts to the steamer and steam the vegetables for an additional 7 to 10 minutes, or until the sprouts are crisp-tender and bright green. Remove the vegetables from the pan and drain. Add the butter or margarine, mustard, salt and pepper to the pan and stir until the butter or margarine has melted. Add the vegetables and cover tightly. Lift up the pan and shake vigorously, holding the cover on, to combine the vegetables and coat them evenly with the butter and mustard mixture. Place in a serving dish and garnish with chopped parsley.

Microwave: To cook 1 pound peeled, trimmed and sliced carrots, place in a covered dish with 2 tablespoons water. Cook on high for 4 to 6 minutes. To cook 1 pound trimmed brussels sprouts, cook in a covered dish with ¼ cup water. Cook on high for 4 to 5 minutes.

Hint: If using large carrots instead of baby ones, cut into half lengthwise; then cut halves into 1½ inch lengths. This is nice to serve at your Thanksgiving dinner or during the holiday season. The vegetables can be cleaned and trimmed a day ahead. The sauce can be made a few hours in advance, however, the vegetables must be cooked shortly before serving.

119

MICROWAVE CARROT AND BROCCOLI PLATTER

2 lbs fresh broccoli
1 lb fresh carrots, peeled and roll-cut
2 T water

Separate broccoli flowerets from stalks. Set aside. Trim 1 inch from ends of stalks and discard. Shred remains of stalks in food processor using shredding disc. Arrange shredded broccoli in center of a 12 or 14-inch round microwave-safe platter. Surround with flowerets. Roll-cut carrots by holding flat on cutting board. Make diagonal cut straight down. Roll carrot a quarter turn and cut again. Pieces should be about 1½ inches long. Arrange near edge of platter around flowerets. Sprinkle water over vegetables. Cover with plastic wrap. Microwave on high 10 to 14 minutes, or until carrots are fork tender, rotating platter two times. Drain. Serve with Microwave Cheese Sauce or browned butter.

Hint: This recipe is so beautiful that it looks like a picture from a magazine. It is so easy to make, can be prepared in advance and always draws raves from everyone who sees and tastes it. Also, it enables you to use the stems of the broccoli which are often discarded.

MICROWAVE CHEESE SAUCE

2 T butter or margarine   ⅛ tsp salt (optional)
⅛ tsp cayenne pepper   2 T flour
1 C shredded Cheddar, Monterey   1 C milk
  Jack or Swiss cheese

Place butter or margarine, salt and cayenne pepper in a one quart bowl. Microwave on high 30 to 45 seconds, or until butter or margarine melts. Blend in flour; stir in milk. Microwave on high 3 to 4 minutes, or until thickened, whisking or stirring after each minute. Add cheese, stirring until melted. Serve over baked potato, fish, vegetables or Microwave Carrot and Broccoli Platter.

Hint: This is where the microwave shows its true colors. If you made this on top of the stove, it would take 2 or 3 times longer for you to stand and stir the sauce.

120

GREEN BEANS AMANDINE

1 lb green beans
2 T butter or margarine
⅓ C slivered almonds, toasted

1 T lemon juice
Salt, to taste

Cook green beans in vegetable steamer until tender. Beans should be bright green and not overcooked. Lightly brown butter or margarine over low heat. Add almonds, lemon juice and salt, to taste. Pour over beans.

Hint: This amandine sauce is also delicious with broccoli, cauliflower or asparagus. To toast almonds, bake at 350° for 3 to 5 minutes, or until golden. Watch carefully or almonds will burn!

PARSLIED GREEN BEANS

1 lb green beans
1 to 1½ T butter or margarine

¼ C fresh parsley, minced
Salt and pepper, to taste

Wash beans and snip off the ends. Cook by dropping into boiling water or placing in vegetable steamer until tender, but still slightly crunchy. Drain well and toss with butter or margarine and parsley. Add salt and pepper to taste.

Hint: This is an easy but delicious way to serve green beans. Green beans are one of the few vegetables that I don't recommend microwaving.

LOW CALORIE OVEN-FRIED EGGPLANT

1 eggplant, peeled	1 T water
Seasoned breadcrumbs	Nonstick cooking spray
1 to 2 egg whites	

Cut eggplant into ½-inch slices. Layer slices in a colander and sprinkle with salt. Allow to drain for 30 minutes. Pat dry. Beat egg whites and water with a fork. Dip eggplant in this mixture. Then dip in bread crumbs. Place on a cookie sheet that has been sprayed with nonstick spray. Bake at 375° or 400° for about 30 minutes, or until eggplant is crispy. Turn over once during baking time.

Hint: By itself, eggplant is very low in calories. However, often it is fried or layered as in traditional fried eggplant with sauce and cheese so it is no longer a low calorie dish. This recipe is low in fat and calories and high in flavor! If you want, sprinkle a little grated Parmesan or shredded Mozzarella to these oven-fried slices during the last few minutes of baking.

RATATOUILLE

2 large onions, sliced	8 to 10 very ripe tomatoes,
4 large garlic cloves, finely chopped	peeled, seeded and chopped
¼ to ½ C olive oil	or 2 to 3 C canned Italian
2 green peppers, peeled and sliced	plum tomatoes
1 large eggplant, diced	Black pepper, to taste
4 or 5 small zucchini, cut into	3 T tomato paste
¼" slices	½ lb mushrooms, sliced (optional)
1½ tsp salt, or to taste	

Saute the onions and garlic in the oil in a large frying pan. When onions are translucent, add the peppers, eggplant, and zucchini and mix well. Reduce the heat, cover the pan tightly and simmer for 10 minutes, shaking the pan or tossing the vegetables two or three times so they cook evenly. Add the tomatoes and the seasonings and continue simmering for another 10 or 12 minutes. Add tomato paste. Uncover the pan and allow the mixture to cook down and the liquid to reduce, stirring frequently. If desired, add mushrooms during the last 5 minutes. This may be served hot or cold.

Hint: This is a wonderful dish to make in late summer and early fall when these vegetables are at their peak, for then they are tastiest and least expensive.

122

ORIENTAL SWEET AND SOUR CABBAGE

2 lbs green cabbage
2 to 3 dried chili peppers, broken
  or 1 tsp chili powder
2 T soy sauce
2 to 3 T canola or peanut oil

2 T white vinegar
2 T sugar
1 tsp salt, or to taste
2 T sesame oil

Cut cabbage into small pieces about 2 inches long and 1 inch wide. Put oil in wok, or frying pan; heat and add cabbage and stir-fry over high heat for about 5 to 10 minutes or until soft. When cabbage is soft, add salt, sugar, soy sauce and dried chili pepper or chili powder. Stir-fry another minute. Add vinegar and sesame oil. Stir until thoroughly mixed.

Hint: This is delicious served hot as a vegetable or served cold as a salad. Instead of cutting cabbage by hand, you can shred it in the food processor by using the shredding disc. Don't worry, if it's more finely shredded than by hand. It will be fine.

SWEET AND SOUR RED CABBAGE

1 small head red cabbage, shredded
4 apples, peeled and thinly sliced
1 to 1½ C cider vinegar

3 T sugar
1 tsp caraway seeds (optional)

Combine all ingredients in a heavy saucepan. Bring to a boil. Cover and reduce heat. Simmer over low heat for 2 hours, adding more vinegar as liquid evaporates.

Hint: Red cabbage and apples are a great tasting, high fiber combination. This recipe is especially nice to make after you've gone apple picking and have made every kind of apple cake, muffin, pie and sauce and are still trying to think of ways to use those apples. This vegetable goes especially well with veal or chicken.

123

Multicolored Baked Peppers

6 large red, green or yellow peppers
1 clove garlic, minced
¼ to ½ C pignolia nuts (pine nuts)
½ C pitted black olives, sliced

¼ C olive oil
½ C flavored bread crumbs
¼ tsp salt
Black pepper, to taste

Cut peppers into strips and place in a greased 2 to 3-quart baking dish. Add everything except bread crumbs and oil. Sprinkle bread crumbs on top and drizzle with oil. Bake uncovered at 350° for 35 to 40 minutes, stirring occasionally.

Hint: This is an unusual and tasty vegetable that looks very attractive, especially at holiday time. It works beautifully as a buffet dish. The dish can be assembled early in the day and baked at serving time. Pignolia, or pine nuts, are usually found in the gourmet or international food sections of most supermarkets or at health food stores.

Grilled Peppers and Onions

2 to 3 peppers, any color, cored and sliced
2 to 3 yellow or red onions, peeled and sliced

Olive oil
Fresh or dried herbs such as oregano, basil or Italian seasoning, to taste

Place peppers and onions on one large piece of heavy duty aluminum foil. Drizzle small amount of oil over them and sprinkle with herbs. Toss, total of 25 to 30 minutes, turning every 5 minutes.

Hint: This method may also be used to grill thinly sliced potatoes, zucchini or summer squash.

*Bring two opposite ends of foil together and fold over tightly. Then seal other two ends tightly.

124

STIR-FRIED PARSNIPS

1 lb parsnips
2 T butter or margarine
1 T fresh gingerroot, grated

Salt and pepper, to taste
3 scallions, chopped

Peel parsnips and cut into 2inch long strips. Heat the butter or margarine in a wok or frying pan until hot. Add parsnips and keep tossing until they begin to brown. Add gingerroot and cook for about 5 more minutes. If parsnips become too brown before they get tender, add ½ cup water and allow it to cook down. Remove from heat and add salt, pepper and scallions.

Hint: This is a tasty way to prepare a vegetable that is often overlooked.

FOUR VEGETABLE PUREE

1 medium potato
1 large carrot
1 stalk celery

1 parsnip
Salt and pepper, to taste
1 T butter or margarine

Peel and slice vegetables. Place in a pan and cover with water. Boil for 10 to 15 minutes, until vegetables are tender. Drain well. Puree in food processor or mash through a sieve. Add butter or margarine and season with salt and pepper.

Hint: You can cook these vegetables in the microwave just until tender, approximately 5 minutes on high. You can also reheat the puree in the microwave or keep it warm over a double boiler which is covered with greased wax paper. This is a delicious change of pace vegetable for fall and winter meals.

125

COOKED PUMPKIN

1 pumpkin   ½ C water

Scrub pumpkin and remove stem. Scrape out pulp and cut into 2-inch chunks. Place pumpkin on foil-lined cookie sheet and pour water around it. Bake at 400° for approximately 35 minutes or until tender. When cool enough to handle, remove pumpkin flesh from skin and mash with a fork or puree in a food processor, using steel blade.

Microwave: Scrub pumpkin and remove stem. Cut in half and scoop out pulp and seeds. Cut into 1½ to 2-inch chunks and add approximately ¼ cup water. Cover with plastic wrap and cook on high for 6 to 8 minutes, or until tender. Drain well and cool slightly. Scrape flesh off skin and mash with a fork or puree in a food processor, using steel blade.

Hint: You can apply the same directions to most varieties of squash such as butternut, spaghetti, acorn, etc. Pumpkin, cooked either way, freezes well and may be frozen in plastic bags or containers for up to 6 months. I usually freeze it in one-cup portions and defrost it as I need it for cakes, breads or muffins.

TOASTED PUMPKIN SEEDS

Remove seeds from pumpkin fibers with your hands and a fork or spoon. Spread on a cookie sheet that has been greased or sprayed with nonstick cooking spray. Sprinkle with salt, to taste. Bake at 350° for 20 to 30 minutes, stirring occasionally, until golden colored.

Microwave: Remove seeds from pumpkin fiber with your hands and a fork or spoon. Spread out seeds in a single layer on a plate. Sprinkle with salt, to taste. Cook on high 1 minute; stir. Cook 30 seconds; stir. Cook 1 to 2 minutes, or until seeds are dry and slightly crisp.

Hint: As you can see, your Halloween pumpkin may be completely recycled, as long as it is cut within 24 hours of having been carved. Just open and remove seeds and cook. In addition to cooking the pumpkin, you can also cook the seeds and have a delicious snack.

GRILLED VEGETABLE MEDLEY

Zucchini
Summer squash
Eggplant
Red onions

Olive oil
Italian seasoning or spices
of your choice

Slice vegetables ½-inch thick. Brush with oil that has had the spices or herbs added to it and place on grill. Cook 4 to 5 minutes on one side and then turn and cook on the other side until just barely charred and tender, approximately 5 minutes.

Hint: This is one of the simplest but most delicious ways to cook vegetables.

YAM PECAN CASSEROLE

BASE:

3½ lbs yams or sweet potatoes
4 T butter or margarine, melted
1 egg, beaten

½ C milk
⅓ C dark brown sugar

TOPPING:

3 T butter or margarine, softened
3 T flour
6 T dark brown sugar
¾ C pecans, coarsely chopped

¼ tsp cinnamon
¼ tsp nutmeg
¼ tsp vanilla

Bake yams or sweet potatoes with skins on at 400° for approximately 40 to 50 minutes, or until tender. Remove from oven and allow to cool. Decrease oven temperature to 375°. Scoop out pulp from cooled yams or potatoes and place in a large bowl. (There should be about 4 cups.) Mash until very smooth. Add melted butter or margarine, egg, brown sugar and milk which has been heated on top of stove or in microwave. Blend well and then spread into a greased 7"x11" casserole dish. Make topping by combining butter or margarine, flour and brown sugar. Add remaining topping ingredients. Sprinkle over yam or potato mixture in casserole. Bake for 30 minutes at 375° or until topping is crusty. Allow to cool 5 minutes before serving.

Microwave: To cook 2 pounds yams or sweet potatoes, prick with tines of a fork, set on paper towel and cook on high for 13 to 15 minutes. If cooking more than 2 pounds, place yams or potatoes in a circular pattern in microwave and adjust time accordingly.

Hint: This casserole may be completely assembled hours before your family or guests sit down to dinner. It is perfect for holiday dinners or buffets.

127

PAGHETTI SQUASH ITALIANO

2 to 3 lbs spaghetti squash
½ to 1 C spaghetti or tomato sauce
½ to 1 C Cheddar or Mozzarella
   cheese, shredded

Microwave: Pierce squash with tines of a long fork. Cook on high 8 to 11 minutes, turning once. When squash is tender, remove from microwave. Cut in half and remove seeds, using tines of fork. Scrape or comb strands of squash so that it resembles spaghetti. Sprinkle with cheese and stir so that cheese melts. Add spaghetti sauce to taste.

Hint: To cook spaghetti squash in a coventional oven, prick it with a long-tined fork and bake at 350˚ for 40 to 80 minutes, depending on the size, until it is tender. Spaghetti squash is very low in calories and is also good with just a little butter or margarine and grated Parmesan cheese or seasoning.

SQUASH IN THE MICROWAVE

Acorn squash: Cut two whole squash in half and cover with plastic wrap. Cook on high 13 to 14 minutes.

Hubbard squash: Cut 2 pounds peeled squash into 1½ to 2-inch chunks. Place in a glass pie plate and cover with plastic wrap. Cook on high 8 to 9 minutes or until tender.

Butternut squash: Cut a 2 lb squash in half and place in a glass pie plate. Cover with plastic wrap and cook for 6 minutes; uncover and cook 6 minutes longer.

Remove squash from skin with a fork and mash. Season with any of the following ingredients or combinations to suit your own taste:

Butter or margarine
Brown sugar
Honey
Salt and pepper
Cinnamon
Powdered ginger
Orange juice
Orange rind
Maple syrup

Hint: If a squash is too hard to cut, place it in the microwave whole, for about 2 minutes. Remove and then cut it in half or cube.

128

Potato Pancakes

4 large potatoes, scrubbed (not peeled)	¾ tsp salt
1 medium onion	Dash pepper
1 egg	2 T flour
1 tsp baking powder	Canola oil

Wash potatoes thoroughly. Grate by hand or use grating or shredding disk of food processor. Let grated potatoes sit for 10 minutes. Then pour them into a colander and press out accumulated liquid. Chop onions by hand or use steel blade of food processor. Add to drained potatoes and stir in egg. Add flour, pepper, salt and baking powder and mix thoroughly. (More liquid will continue to form, but don't pour it off.) Occasionally stir mixture as you remove spoonfuls for frying. Drop the batter by tablespoons into a large frying pan (an electric frying pan is very handy) containing ¼-inch hot oil. Flatten pancakes with a metal spatula. When edges become brown, turn and brown other side. Drain on paper towels and keep warm in a low oven until ready to serve. Serve with sour cream or apple sauce.

Yield: approximately 24 pancakes

Hint: *These may be made into tiny pancakes for hors d'oeuvres or larger ones to serve as an accompaniment to a meal.*

Low Calorie Potato Chips

4 medium potatoes	Salt and pepper, to taste
Nonstick cooking spray	

Scrub and slice potatoes very thinly. Place on a baking sheet that has been sprayed with nonstick cooking spray. Bake, turning once, at 450° for 30 to 40 minutes, or until potatoes are crispy. Season with salt and pepper.

Hint: *Whoever heard of potato chips without fat or guilt?*

VEN FRENCH FRIES

3 large potatoes
1 T olive or canola oil

1 T cold water
Salt and herbs, to taste

Scrub potatoes but do not peel. Cut into ½-inch sticks. Combine oil and water in a bowl. Add potato sticks and mix until well coated. Spray a roasting pan with nonstick cooking spray or brush the pan with oil. Spread potatoes in a single layer in pan. Sprinkle with salt. Bake at 475° for 30 minutes or until browned, turning occasionally.

Hint: These French fries are very healthy because the skin is a good source of dietary fiber and the recipe contains very little fat. You can eliminate the salt by adding herbs and spices such as garlic, oregano and basil while the potatoes are roasting.

Pasta and Rice

FETTUCINE ALFREDO

1 C medium or heavy cream
1 C Parmesan cheese, freshly grated
1 stick unsalted butter
1 lb fettucine, cooked and drained

Salt, to taste
White pepper, to taste
Extra Parmesan cheese

Combine cream, Parmesan cheese and butter in a double boiler and cook just until melted. Pour over hot pasta and toss until well combined. Add salt and white pepper, to taste. Serve with additional Parmesan, if desired.

Microwave: Combine butter, Parmesan cheese and cream. Cook on medium for 4 to 6 minutes, or until cheese is melted.

Hint: This has been a favorite in our house for years, except when we are dieting! This is one recipe that is worth the calories and fat. It's also very easy to prepare. Serve with a salad and Italian bread.

SHORT CUT SPINACH LASAGNA

2 C (1 lb) low fat or nonfat
cottage cheese
2 C (½ lb) part skim shredded
Mozzarella cheese, divided
1 egg or egg substitute
10 oz pkg frozen chopped spinach

1 tsp oregano
Salt and pepper, to taste
29 to 32 oz spaghetti sauce
9 lasagna noodles (½ lb),
uncooked
1 C water

Thaw and drain spinach. In large bowl combine cottage cheese, 1 cup of the Mozzarella, egg, spinach, salt, oregano and pepper. In greased 9"x13" baking dish, layer 1 cup sauce, third of noodles and half the cheese mixture. Repeat. Top with remaining noodles, then remaining sauce. Sprinkle with remaining 1 cup Mozzarella. Pour water around edges. Cover tightly with foil. Bake at 350° for one hour and 15 minutes or until bubbly. Let stand 15 minutes before serving.

Hint: This is a wonderful low cholesterol, low fat pasta dish that appeals to people of all ages. It is especially appealing to the cook, because it is so quick and easy to make! You don't even have to cook the lasagna first, which saves both time and mess. This may be made up to 2 days in advance. It also freezes very well.

131

TOFU LASAGNA

½ lb mushrooms, sliced
3 cloves garlic, minced
2 to 3 T olive oil
1 C firm tofu
¼ C fresh Parmesan cheese, grated
¼ C fresh parsley, chopped

1 lb low fat or nonfat cottage
  cheese
9 lasagna noodles (½ lb)
3 C spaghetti sauce
8 oz part skim Mozzarella
  cheese, shredded

Sauté mushrooms and garlic in olive oil. Mash tofu with a fork or shred in a food processor. Combine tofu, Parmesan cheese, cottage cheese and parsley. Add mushroom mixture. Boil and drain lasagna noodles. Make lasagna by layering the ingredients in a greased 9"x13" baking pan in the following order:

1) 1 C spaghetti sauce
2) 3 lasagna noodles
3) ⅓ tofu mixture
4) ⅓ pkg (about 2⅔ oz) Mozzarella

Repeat two more times, ending with cheese on top. Bake at 350° for 45 minutes. Allow to stand for a few minutes before cutting.

Hint: Even if you think you don't like tofu you'll probably like this, especially since the tofu is grated and really unidentifiable. The secret is not to tell people until after they have eaten it! Since most of us no longer have the time to make our own spaghetti sauce, any commercially prepared sauce is fine.

ORZO AND ONIONS

2 qts water
½ tsp salt, or to taste
2 medium onions, chopped

1 C orzo (pasta)
2 to 3 T butter or margarine
Salt and pepper, to taste

Bring water and salt to a boil. Add orzo and cook for about 12 minutes or until tender. Drain. Melt butter or margarine in a pan and saute onions for about 4 to 5 minutes. Add orzo to the cooked onions and stir well. Season to taste.

Hint: Orzo is a small rice-shaped pasta that seems to have its own character. It isn't like rice and yet it isn't like most pastas. Try it, you'll like it!

PESTO SAUCE

2 C fresh basil leaves, stems
  trimmed and packed
2 large (or 4 to 5 small)
  garlic cloves

½ C pine nuts or walnuts
¾ C freshly grated Parmesan
  cheese
⅔ C olive oil

Place the basil, garlic and pine nuts or walnuts in a blender or a food processor using the steel blade. Blend until smooth. Add the cheese and oil and blend again. Transfer to a container and pour a thin layer of olive oil on top. Cover and refrigerate.

Yield: 1 cup

Hint: Pesto may be used to dress both hot and cold pasta. Dilute pesto with 2 tablespoons of the cooking liquid before tossing with hot pasta. It may also be blended with sour cream or yogurt to spread on fish or chicken. It's great on baked potatoes or as a garnish for Minestrone Soup (pg. 26). Also, pesto may be mixed with a little butter or margarine, brushed on French bread, wrapped in foil and heated in the oven at 350° for 3 to 5 minutes. Pesto sauce will keep frozen up to 3 months.

LINGUINE WITH BROCCOLI

½ lb linguine or thin spaghetti,
  broken into thirds or fourths
2 13¾ oz cans chicken broth or
  27½ oz homemade chicken broth
2 T olive or canola oil

4 garlic cloves, minced
Dash cayenne pepper
1 bunch broccoli, mostly
  flowerets
Parmesan cheese, for garnish

Brown garlic in oil in a large pot. Add chicken broth and cayenne pepper. When broth boils, add linguine and broccoli. Cover and cook for 10 to 12 minutes, stirring often so that linguine doesn't stick to the pot. Serve immediately and garnish with freshly grated Parmesan cheese.

Hint: This is a great combination that is easy to prepare. Everything for this dish can be assembled in advance; however, it tastes best when eaten immediately.

133

134

PANISH SPAGHETTI

1 onion, diced
1 green pepper, diced
3 stalks celery, diced
1 T olive or canola oil
16 oz can tomatoes
6 oz can tomato paste
1 T sugar

Salt and pepper, to taste
1 lb thin spaghetti
½ C Cheddar or Mozzarella
   cheese, shredded
¼ to ½ C Parmesan cheese,
   grated

Saute onion, pepper and celery in oil until soft. Add tomatoes, tomato paste, sugar, salt and pepper. Stir. Cook spaghetti in salted water and drain. In a large casserole, mix spaghetti with tomato mixture. Combine cheeses and sprinkle over top. Bake at 350° for about 35 to 40 minutes, or until cheese is brown.

Hint: *This is a tasty and colorful dish that, when served with a salad and fresh bread, could stand alone as an economical (protein and cost-wise) meal. You could also use it as a side dish for almost any meal.*

ARLEY AND MUSHROOM PILAF

4 T olive or canola oil
½ lb mushrooms, sliced
1 large onion, diced
1 C pearl barley
2½ C chicken or beef broth

½ tsp rosemary
½ tsp marjoram
Black pepper, to taste
Chopped parsley, for garnish

Heat oil in an ovenproof casserole. Add mushrooms and onion; saute until soft. Add barley, broth and seasonings. Bring to a boil. Cover and simmer for 40 to 45 minutes or bake in oven at 350° for 1 hour or until all liquid has been absorbed. Garnish with chopped parsley.

Hint: *Barley is one of the most nutritious grains. It contains protein, is low in fat and is a good source of water soluble fiber which is believed to help reduce cholesterol. It has a mild nutty taste and a slightly chewy texture. This recipe is a delightful alternative to rice and pasta. My children love it, however, minus the mushrooms. It is delicious with or without mushrooms!*

Lo MEIN

½ lb (½ pkg) fresh Chinese noodles

1½ oz fresh Shitake mushrooms, thinly sliced or 3 Chinese dried mushrooms, soaked, drained and sliced

1 tsp fresh ginger, finely minced

1 C chopped scallions, divided

2 C Chinese cabbage, thinly sliced

½ red pepper, thinly sliced

1 C bean sprouts

1 to 2 T peanut or canola oil

2 to 3 tsp sesame oil, divided

SAUCE:

4 T soy sauce

2 T dry sherry

2 tsp sugar

½ tsp Five Spice powder

Boil 10 cups of water. Put noodles in boiling water; wait for second boil. Then remove noodles and drain. Fill the empty pot with water and swish noodles in it and drain again. Toss noodles with 1 to 2 teaspoons sesame oil. Set aside. Place wok over high heat and add 1 to 2 tablespoons peanut or canola oil. When oil is hot, add ginger and half the scallions and stir-fry for 1 minute. Add cabbage, red pepper, mushrooms and bean sprouts. Stir-fry for 2 minutes. Pour sauce over vegetables. Add reserved noodles, remaining half cup of scallions and a few drops sesame oil. Heat until hot, about 3 minutes.

Hint: The other half of the package of Chinese noodles can be frozen for future use. It is important to rinse the noodles well to remove the excess starch. Spaghetti may be substitued for the fresh noodles. Leftover beef, chicken, pork or shrimp may be added to the lo mein. Five Spice powder can be found in the oriental section in most supermarkets.

136

CHINESE FRIED RICE

3 T canola or peanut oil, divided
3 eggs, beaten
4 scallions, chopped
2 large onions, chopped
4 C cold cooked rice
½ lb bean sprouts
3 to 4 T oyster sauce

¼ C dried Chinese mushrooms
   (black) that have been soaked,
   drained and sliced or 1 C fresh
   Shitake mushrooms, sliced
2 T soy sauce, or to taste and for
   desired color
½ T sesame oil

Heat wok or large frying pan and add 1 tablespoon oil. Add eggs and beat with a whisk to scramble. Scramble until dry. Remove. Heat 1 to 2 tablespoons oil in wok or frying pan and add onions and scallions. Stir-fry until soft. Then add rice and stir-fry for a few minutes or until rice is separated. Add bean sprouts, mushrooms, reserved scrambled egg, oyster sauce and soy sauce. Mix well. Just before serving, add sesame oil.

Hint: The secret to making traditional Chinese fried rice is to use cold cooked rice. This is a great way to use leftover rice. The oyster sauce, sesame oil, soy sauce and dried mushrooms are available in the oriental section of most supermarkets. Leftover beef, chicken, pork and shrimp may be added to the rice.

CURRIED RICE

1 C raw rice
3 to 4 T butter or margarine
2 C chicken bouillon
½ C raisins

½ C onion, chopped
1 to 2 tsp curry
1½ tsp salt, or to taste
½ C flaked coconut

Saute onion and rice in butter or margarine until golden. Add curry and mix well. Add remaining ingredients. Bring to a boil and then simmer for 20 minutes, or until liquid is absorbed.

Hint: This rice goes especially well with a meat or poultry dish that has any form of fruit in it.

RICE PILAF

1 to 2 T butter, margarine,
olive or canola oil
½ C raw rice
½ C fine noodles, crushed

1½ C hot chicken or beef broth
¼ C blanched almonds, sautéed
in 1 T butter or margarine (optional)

Melt butter or margarine, or heat oil, in a 2-quart saucepan or casserole. Sauté noodles and rice until golden in color. Add broth and boil. Reduce heat and cover. Simmer over low heat until all liquid is absorbed, approximately 25 to 30 minutes. If desired, sprinkle with sautéed almonds.

Hint: This is an easy recipe that goes well with most everything - poultry, beef, lamb and seafood. It may be made several hours in advance and reheated in the oven.

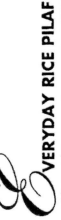

EVERYDAY RICE PILAF

1 T olive or canola oil
1 T butter or margarine
1 large onion, diced

1 C raw rice
2½ C chicken broth
2 T parsley, minced (optional)

Heat butter or margarine and oil in a 2-quart saucepan or casserole. Add onion and sauté until limp. Add rice and saute just until rice and onions begin to take on a golden color. Add chicken broth and boil. Cover and reduce heat. Simmer for 25 minutes, or until all the broth has been absorbed. Garnish with chopped parsley, if desired.

Hint: This is called Everyday Rice Pilaf because it's so easy to make that you can make it everyday.

137

 RANGE RICE

1 onion, chopped
¼ C celery leaves, chopped
2 to 3 T butter or margarine
1 C long grain rice
1 C chicken broth

1 C orange juice
1 tsp orange rind, freshly grated
¼ tsp thyme
1 T parsley, or to taste
Salt and pepper, to taste

Saute onion and celery leaves in butter or margarine until soft. Add remaining ingredients. Cover and simmer for 20 to 25 minutes, or until liquid is absorbed.

Hint: This rice is delicious on its own, or it may be used as a stuffing for chicken, duck or Cornish Hens with Apricot Sauce (pg. 109).

138

Desserts

JIFFY BLUEBERRY SAUCE

2 C blueberries	3 T sugar
2 T fresh lemon juice	2 tsp cornstarch

Combine all ingredients and place in a saucepan. Cook over moderately high heat, stirring occasionally, until mixture is hot and begins to thicken. Sauce will thicken as it cools.

Microwave: Combine all ingredients and place in a large glass bowl. Cover with plastic wrap, which has one hole poked in it. Cook on high for 3 minutes, stirring once or twice during cooking. Sauce will thicken as it cools.

Hint: Serve hot with pancakes or waffles or at room temperature or chilled over ice cream or frozen yogurt. Raspberries, strawberries or any other berries may be used to make this sauce. Also, you can use frozen berries, however increase the cooking time.

POACHED PEACHES

2½ lbs ripe peaches (8 to 9)	1 C water
¾ C sugar	Zest of 1 orange or lemon, grated
1 C white wine (Chablis,	1 stick cinnamon
Chardonnay, Savignon blanc)	

First remove skin from peaches by plunging them into boiling water for about 40 seconds. Remove with a slotted spoon and immediately plunge into ice cold water. Using a sharp paring knife, peel off skin. Cut peaches in half and remove pits. Place peaches and everything except wine in saucepan and bring to a boil. Reduce heat and simmer for 15 minutes. Add wine and cook for 10 to 15 more minutes or until peaches are tender. Cool and chill until serving time. Garnish with mint leaves, raspberries and/or whipped cream.

Hint: This is a wonderful dessert to make when peaches are in season. You can make it a day or two in advance. It contains no fat. Zinfandel or blush wine may be substituted for white wine. To get the zest (skin) of the orange or lemon without getting the bitter white pith below it, use a lemon zester. Zesters are available at most kitchen equipment shops.

139

PEACH MELBA

10 oz pkg frozen, lightly sweetened
  raspberries, defrosted
1 T cornstarch
5 to 6 fresh peaches or canned
  sliced peaches

2 T water
2 T lemon juice
1 qt vanilla ice cream or
  frozen yogurt

Place raspberries in a small saucepan. Combine cornstarch and water to make a paste and stir into raspberries. Place over moderate heat and stir constantly until thickened and clear. Let cool. Peel and slice the peaches. Sprinkle with lemon juice to keep from discoloring. To serve, place a scoop of ice cream in five or six fruit dishes or stemmed glasses. Arrange peach slices around the ice cream and top with raspberry sauce.

Yield: 5 or 6 servings

Microwave: Combine raspberries, cornstarch and water. Cover with plastic wrap which has one hole poked through. Cook on high for 2½ to 3 minutes, stirring once or twice during cooking. Sauce will thicken as it cools.

Hint: *If made with frozen yogurt, this is a low fat dessert that is attractive and delicious.*

MERINGUE GLACEES

3 egg whites
Pinch salt

1 C sugar

Beat egg whites and salt until foamy. Add sugar gradually and beat until stiff and shiny. Line cookie sheets with parchment paper, brown paper or pans that have been greased and dusted with flour. Shape meringue with spoon or pastry bag into five 3½inch cups or glacees. Bake at 250° for 40 minutes. Remove from paper or cookie sheet at once and place on a rack to cool.

Yield: 5 glacees

Hint: *Glacees may be made several days in advance and kept fresh in an airtight tin. They may be filled with ice cream or frozen yogurt, and topped with Peach Melba, Jiffy Blueberry Sauce (pg. 139), Hot Fudge Sauce (pg. 142), Raspberry Orange Sauce (pg. 141) or liqueur of your choice.*

140

CRANBERRY MICROWAVE TOPPING

½ C sugar
½ C light corn syrup

2 C cranberries

Combine sugar, corn syrup and cranberries in a 1-quart bowl. Cover tightly and microwave on high for 4 minutes; stir. Cover and microwave until sugar dissolves and mixture boils, 2 to 3 minutes longer.

Hint: Serve over ice cream or frozen yogurt

RASPBERRY ORANGE SAUCE

10 oz pkg frozen raspberries, defrosted
¼ C orange liqueur

11 oz can mandarin oranges, drained

Combine in a tightly covered container and marinate in the refrigerator for at least 24 hours. Serve over vanilla ice cream or frozen yogurt.

Hint: To make this fancier, place ice cream on a slice of pound cake or on a meringue glacee and pour topping over it.

TROPICAL FRUIT SALAD DRESSING OR DIP

1 C sour cream or plain yogurt
¼ C grated coconut
¼ to ⅓ C apricot jam

½ C macadamia nuts or walnuts, chopped

Whisk together all ingredients and serve as a sauce or dip for fresh fruit.

Hint: To make this dip creamier, use the steel blade of your food processor to chop the nuts. Then add the jam and coconut and process for only 10 to 20 seconds, or until lumps are removed from jam. Fold in sour cream or yogurt and process just until combined.

FRESH FRUIT DIP

8 oz cream cheese, softened   7½ oz jar Marshmallow Fluff

Mix in electric mixer until light and fluffy.

Hint: This combination, as strange as it may sound, is fabulous! You can serve it in a small cantaloupe or grapefruit half that you have zigzag cut with a paring knife or decorating knife. Use a grapefruit knife to scoop out the flesh of the fruit and then fill with the dip. If you like, tint the dip with food coloring to coordinate with your color scheme.

HOT FUDGE SAUCE

5 oz unsweetened chocolate
¼ lb butter
12 oz can evaporated milk

1 lb confectioners' sugar
½ to 1 tsp salt
1½ tsp vanilla

Melt chocolate and butter over a double boiler. Add all remaining ingredients except vanilla. Cook for 8 minutes. Add vanilla and mix well. Serve over ice cream or ice cream pie.

Hint: This may be the recipe of a famous Boston ice cream company. The sauce will keep in a jar in the refrigerator for a few weeks. Reheat as needed.

BRICKLE ICE CREAM PIE

1 pkg ladyfingers (sponge cake cookies)
2 qts coffee ice cream
1 qt chocolate ice cream

6 oz pkg Bits'O Brickle, crushed
¼ C coffee liqueur (optional)
Whipped cream
Chocolate sprinkles or shavings

Line sides of a 9-inch springform pan with ladyfingers. Soften ice creams and blend together. Fold Bits'O Brickle and coffee liqueur into ice cream. Pour into ladyfinger-lined pan. Freeze for 24 hours or more. Decorate with whipped cream, sprinkles, etc. Remove from springform to serve.

Hint: If Bits'O Brickle is not available, Skor or Heath Bar candy bars may be crushed and substituted. You can make this dessert several days in advance and put it in the freezer. It serves a large crowd.

142

SHERBET WATERMELON BOAT

1 pt lime sherbet
1 pt lemon sherbet or
vanilla ice cream

1 qt raspberry sherbet
1 C mini chocolate chips

Using a triple layer of heavy duty foil, fold to resemble the shape of a watermelon. Spray foil with nonstick cooking spray. Spread lime sherbet over bottom and slightly up the sides of the foil to resemble the skin of the watermelon. Freeze until firm. Then spread lemon sherbet or vanilla ice cream as next layer and freeze. Soften raspberry sherbet so that chocolate chips can be folded in to resemble seeds. Spread over previous layer and shape to resemble a watermelon. Freeze until serving time. Slice to serve.

Hint: This is a very pretty and refreshing spring and summer dessert that you can make up to a week in advance.

CHOCOLATE MOUSSE

4 eggs, separated
6 oz chocolate chips
⅓ C hot coffee

1½ T rum or orange liqueur,
coffee liqueur, etc.
Whipped cream, for garnish

Whip egg whites until stiff but not dry. Place chocolate chips and coffee in blender or food processor using steel blade. Mix until chips dissolve. Add egg yolks and rum or liqueur. Fold a quarter of whites into chocolate mixture. Transfer to a bowl and fold in remaining whites. Spoon into small ramekins, Chocolate Cups (pg. 144) or into a large serving bowl. Chill at least 2 to 3 hours before serving. If desired, garnish with whipped cream.

Hint: This is one of the easiest and best tasting recipes for chocolate mousse. It is especially great for last minute guests because it only takes a few minutes to make and a few hours to chill. It can also be made a day in advance.

CHOCOLATE CUPS ROYALE

CHOCOLATE CUPS:

6 oz semi-sweet chocolate   2 T butter or margarine

Melt chocolate and butter or margarine in a double boiler or microwave just until melted and smooth. With a small spatula quickly spread the chocolate around the inside of a doubled paper or foil baking cup until the paper is covered with chocolate. Place in a cupcake pan or a 6-ounce custard cup and chill in refrigerator until firm. When ready to serve, remove from refrigerator and peel paper or foil off so that a free-standing chocolate cup remains.

Yield: 6 cups

FILLING:

Few pieces sponge cake or ladyfingers, cut into rounds just the size of the bottom of the chocolate cups

1½ C fresh fruit, cut up (orange, melon, pineapple, bananas, berries)

3 to 4 T orange liqueur
2 T sugar
Vanilla ice cream
Whipped cream
6 strawberries or raspberries

Sprinkle each sponge cake round with 1 to 2 teaspoons orange liqueur and place in the bottom of each chocolate cup. Cover with a small scoop (or spoon) of vanilla ice cream. Cover with fresh fruit and top with whipped cream and a fresh strawberry or raspberry.

Hint: The chocolate cups may also be filled with just ice cream, frozen yogurt, sherbert or chocolate mousse.

144

COFFEE NUT TORTONI

1 C whipping cream
¼ C sugar
1 T instant coffee
1 tsp vanilla
Few drops almond extract
1 egg white
2 T sugar

¼ C almonds, toasted and finely
   chopped
¼ C flaked coconut, toasted and
   crumbled
Maraschino cherries, for
   garnish (optional)

Whip cream until it has a spreadable consistency, but not quite stiff. Fold in sugar, coffee and flavorings. Beat egg white until soft peaks form; gradually add 2 tablespoons sugar and beat to stiff peaks. Combine almonds and coconut. Fold egg white and half the nut mixture into whipped cream. Spoon into eight ramekins or paper baking cups set into muffin tins. Sprinkle remaining nut mixture on top. Freeze until firm. Garnish each with one maraschino cherry, if desired.

Yield: 8 tortoni

Hint: This goes well with an Italian meal. You can make it several days in advance. To toast almonds and coconut, bake at 350° for 3 to 4 minutes, or until golden.

GRAPES ROCKEFELLER

1 lb red, green or black
   seedless grapes
1 C sour cream or plain yogurt

¼ to ⅓ C brown sugar
Mint sprigs, for garnish

Remove stems from grapes. Wash and drain well. Whisk brown sugar into sour cream or yogurt, mixing well so as to remove lumps from brown sugar. Fold in drained grapes. Garnish with sprigs of fresh mint, if desired.

Hint: Blueberries, strawberries, peaches or a combination of fruits taste wonderful in this sauce.

STRAWBERRIES ROMANOFF

1 qt strawberries
Sugar, to taste
½ pt vanilla ice cream, softened
½ C whipping cream

2 to 3 T cherry (Kirsch) or
   orange liqueur
Mint sprigs, for garnish

Wash, hull, slice and sugar berries. Add liqueur and refrigerate for a few hours. Whip cream and fold together with softened ice cream. Lightly fold in the berries and refrigerate until serving time, at least one hour. Garnish with fresh mint, if desired.

Hint: This is a simple, delicious and beautiful dessert. If served in champagne glasses, it is especially elegant.

CRANBERRY APPLE SAUCE

1 T butter or margarine
1 lb cranberries, fresh or frozen
6 small or 3 large apples,
   peeled and cubed

1½ C brown sugar
1 T cornstarch
1 tsp cinnamon
½ tsp cloves (optional)

Melt butter or margarine, add cranberries and apples. Saute until half done. Mix sugar, cornstarch and spices and pour over fruit. Mix well and cook over low heat for about 30 minutes or until berries pop and apples are tender.

Microwave: Place all ingredients in a large microwave-safe bowl. Cover with plastic wrap which has one hole poked in it. Cook on high, stirring once, for approximately 8 minutes or until fruit is tender.

Hint: You can serve this sauce for dessert or use it as an accompaniment to turkey, chicken or pork.

Microwave Fresh Fruit Betty

6 to 7 large apples, nectarines, peaches or pears (or combination)
¼ C raisins
1 T lemon juice
1½ C flour
¾ C light brown sugar, firmly packed
1 tsp cinnamon
½ tsp ginger (optional)
⅛ tsp mace (optional)
½ C butter or margarine, softened

Peel fruit and remove seeds or pits. Cut into thin slices. Place fruit in a 9-inch pie plate. Sprinkle with raisins and lemon juice. Combine flour, brown sugar and spices. Add butter or margarine. Blend until well mixed and crumbly. Spread over fruit, patting firmly into place. Cook on high for 10 to 12 minutes or until fruit is tender, rotating plate a half turn after 5 minutes. Cool for 10 minutes. Serve warm. Top with vanilla ice cream, frozen yogurt or whipped cream.

Hint: This is especially delicious in late summer and early fall when these fruits are in season. A combination of apples and peaches is marvelous! If you don't have a microwave, just bake in a conventional oven at 350° for about 30 to 40 minutes, or until fruit is tender and top is golden.

Lowfat Apple Crisp

4 C apples, peeled and sliced
1 T lemon juice
2 T flour
6 T brown sugar, divided
¼ C water
2 T margarine, melted
½ C oatmeal
1 tsp cinnamon

Toss apples with lemon juice, flour and 2 tablespoons of brown sugar. Pour into a 1-quart baking dish that has been sprayed with nonstick cooking spray. Add water. Combine margarine, remaining brown sugar, oatmeal and cinnamon. Spread over the apples. Bake at 350° for about 25 minutes, or until apples are tender.

Hint: This is a quick, tasty and healthy family dessert that can bake along with your meal or bake while you are eating dinner.

147

PEACHES OR PEARS WITH MACAROONS AND APRICOT GLAZE

12 canned peach or pear halves	4 T butter or margarine
8 macaroons, crumbled	4 T brown sugar
1 C apricot jam	3 to 4 T orange liqueur
2 T lemon juice	or orange juice

Place the drained peach halves in a greased 9"x13" pan. Combine lemon juice with margarine and brown sugar and heat until sugar is dissolved. Place a teaspoonful over each peach or pear half. Fill cavities with macaroon crumbs. Heat apricot jam with orange liqueur and drizzle a little over each peach half. Bake at 350° for 15 to 20 minutes or until heated through.

Hint: *This dessert is nice and light after a big meal. It can be used on Passover, especially for those on low cholesterol diets.*

GRAPENUT PUDDING

1 C sugar	1 T lemon rind
1 T flour	3 eggs, unbeaten
6 T grapenuts	2 C milk
2 T butter or margarine, melted	Whipped cream, for garnish
1½ T lemon juice	

Combine sugar, flour and grapenuts. Stir in margarine or butter, lemon juice and rind. Fold in eggs, one at a time. Stir in milk slowly. Pour into a well greased 1½ quart pan. Place in larger ovenproof pan with ½-inch water. Bake at 375° for 1 hour. Cool and then refrigerate until serving time. Garnish with whipped cream, if desired.

Hint: *This recipe is a good way to disguise healthy food. Grapenuts, a wheat and barley cereal, is a good source of fiber and the milk is a good source of calcium.*

Cakes and Pies

APPLE OR PEACH TORTE

CRUST:

1 C butter or margarine
⅔ C sugar

1 tsp vanilla
2 C flour

FILLING:

8 oz cream cheese, softened
¼ C sugar

1 tsp vanilla
1 egg

TOPPING:

4 C apples or peaches, peeled and
sliced
⅓ C sugar

1 tsp cinnamon
Lemon juice

GLAZE:

Apricot jam (approximately ½ C)

Cream butter or margarine with sugar until fluffy. Add vanilla and flour and mix until well blended. Press into bottom and a little way up the sides of a 9-inch springform pan. Cream filling ingredients together and pour into crust. Drizzle lemon juice over fruit and then mix fruit with sugar and cinnamon. Arrange apples or peaches attractively on top of filling. Bake at 350° for about 1 hour, or until golden. Glaze with apricot jam that has been melted and strained. Chill for a few hours. Remove from the refrigerator about 30 minutes before serving.

Hint: This is a very fancy looking dessert that is easy to prepare. It is delicious with either apples or peaches or a combination. I like to make it in late summer or early fall when these fruits are at their peak. You can peel peaches by dropping them into boiling water for about 40 to 60 seconds. Remove with a slotted spoon and place in cold water for the same length of time. Then remove skin with a sharp paring knife. This technique can also be used to peel tomatoes.

FRESH APPLE CAKE

4 medium apples
2 C sugar
4 eggs
1 C oil
¼ C sugar, mixed with 1 tsp cinnamon
3 C flour, sifted

1 T baking powder
½ C orange juice
½ tsp salt
1 tsp vanilla
Confectioners' sugar, for sprinkling on top

Grease and flour a 10-inch tube pan. Slice apples. Beat eggs, gradually beat in sugar, then oil. Resift flour with baking powder and salt, add to beaten mixture in small amounts, alternately with orange juice. Beat in vanilla. Pour about one quarter of the batter into prepared pan. Arrange apple slices on top and sprinkle a little cinnamon-sugar mixture on apples. Repeat these layers using about a quarter of the batter each time. Make last layer batter. Bake at 350° for one hour. Cool and remove from pan. Sprinkle confectioners' sugar on top.

Hint: This cake is a favorite in our house during apple season. It goes well with coffee or tea for dessert or brunch. It freezes well.

PEACH KUCHEN

2 C flour
¼ tsp baking powder
½ tsp salt
1 C sugar (reserve 2 T)
½ C butter or margarine

12 peach halves (fresh or canned)
1 tsp cinnamon
2 egg yolks
1 C sour cream

Sift together flour, baking powder, salt and 2 tablespoons sugar. With a pastry blender or food processor, blend in butter or margarine until it resembles cornmeal. Pile into an ungreased 8-inch square pan or springform pan and pat an even layer of crumbs on bottom and half way up sides of pan. Place peach halves on pastry. Combine sugar and cinnamon and sprinkle over peaches. Bake at 400° for 15 minutes. Combine egg yolks with sour cream and pour over kuchen and bake 30 minutes longer. Cool on a wire rack.

Hint: This is especially delicious during peach season when you can use fresh peaches. It's very impressive looking, but so simple to make.

150

BANANA CAKE

1 stick butter or margarine
1¼ C sugar
2 eggs
1 tsp vanilla
2 large very ripe bananas
1 tsp baking soda
¾ C plain yogurt
1 tsp baking powder

2 C flour
⅓ C mini-chocolate chips
   (optional)
⅓ C walnuts, coarsely
   chopped (optional)
Confectioners' sugar, for
   sprinkling on top

Cream butter or margarine with sugar until fluffy. Add eggs and vanilla and blend well. Add bananas, which have been well mashed or finely pureed in a food processor. Dissolve baking soda in yogurt and let stand for at least 2 to 3 minutes. Yogurt will double in volume so use a 2-cup measure. Add to batter. Then add flour and baking powder. Mix well. Fold in chocolate chips and/or walnuts, if desired. Bake at 350° in a greased and floured 9-inch square pan for 45 to 50 minutes or until toothpick, inserted in center, comes out clean. Cool 10 minutes. Remove from pan. Sprinkle with confectioners' sugar.

Hint: This recipe is good for using overripe bananas. It is a moist cake that freezes well.

BLUEBERRY CAKE

2 C sugar
2 sticks butter or margarine
2 eggs
1 C milk
2½ tsp baking powder
2 tsp vanilla

1 to 2 tsp cinnamon
2½ C blueberries
3 C flour
½ tsp salt
Confectioners' sugar, for
   sprinkling on top

Cream sugar and butter or margarine until fluffy. Beat in eggs, milk, flour, baking powder, salt, cinnamon and vanilla. Fold in blueberries. Bake in a greased and floured 9"x13" pan at 350° for 35 minutes. Increase oven to 375° and bake another 5 to 7 minutes, or until golden and cake tester or toothpick, inserted in center, comes out clean. Cool and cut into squares. Sprinkle with confectioners' sugar.

Hint: This cake melts in your mouth and always receives raves! It's great for barbecues and picnics because it yields a large amount and travels well. It also freezes well. You can substitute raspberries for blueberries.

ERMAN BLUEBERRY KUCHEN

1½ C flour, sifted
Dash salt
4 C (1½ pts) blueberries
3 T quick-cooking tapioca
⅛ tsp cinnamon
1 C sugar, divided

½ C butter or margarine, softened
1 T fresh lemon juice
¼ tsp salt
Whipped cream, vanilla ice cream or vanilla frozen yogurt

Combine flour, ½ cup sugar, dash salt and butter or margarine. Mix with pastry blender or fork until crumbs form. Measure ¾ cup of mixture and set aside. Press remaining crumbs over bottom and about ¾ inch up the sides of a 9-inch springform pan. Combine blueberries, lemon juice, ½ cup sugar, tapioca, salt and cinnamon. Let stand for 15 minutes. Spoon blueberry mixture into crumb-lined pan. Bake at 425° for 20 minutes. Then sprinkle with the ¾ cup reserved crumbs. Bake 20 to 25 minutes longer, or until crumbs are golden. Serve warm or at room temperature. Serve with whipped cream, vanilla ice cream, or vanilla frozen yogurt.

Hint: Although this looks like a very fancy tart, it is simple to make! It also contains no cholesterol.

ONEY CAKE

1 C honey
1 C sugar
¾ C oil
3 eggs
Rinds of 1 lemon and 1 orange, finely chopped
¼ tsp allspice
1 tsp cinnamon

Pinch salt
3½ C flour
1½ tsp baking powder
1½ tsp baking soda
1 C strong coffee
½ C walnuts, coarsely chopped
¼ C raisins, dusted with flour

Sift flour, baking powder and baking soda together and set aside. With mixer at medium speed, mix honey, sugar, oil and eggs together. Add lemon and orange rinds, allspice, cinnamon and salt. Add reserved dry ingredients. Add coffee and then fold in nuts and raisins. Pour into a greased and floured 10-inch tube pan and bake at 350° for 55 to 60 minutes, or until toothpick, inserted in center, comes out clean.

Hint: This may also be baked in two 9"x5" loaf pans at 350° for 40 to 45 minutes. This cake freezes well so if you're not having a big crowd make one for now and freeze the other for later or give it as a gift.

ARROT CAKE

2 C flour
2 C sugar
2 tsp baking powder
2 tsp baking soda
⅔ tsp cinnamon

1 tsp salt
4 eggs
1½ C canola oil
3 C carrots, finely grated
½ C walnuts, chopped

Combine all dry ingredients. Beat eggs and oil together and fold in dry ingredients. Add carrots and nuts. Pour into three greased 9-inch pans. Bake at 300° for 45 minutes and then increase to 350° for 25 to 30 minutes, or until a toothpick, inserted in center, comes out clean. Cool on wire rack.

FROSTING:

8 oz pkg cream cheese, softened
1 stick butter or margarine, softened

1 lb confectioners' sugar
1 tsp vanilla
Walnut halves, for garnish

Beat the cream cheese and butter or margarine until fluffy. Add sugar and vanilla and mix well. Frost between layers and around sides and top of cake. Garnish with walnut halves.

Hint: This carrot cake may be made in advance or frozen. However, it is not advisable to freeze it frosted. You can use a food processor to grate the carrots and chop the walnuts.

HERRY SQUARES

¾ C butter or margarine
1 C sugar
2 eggs
2 C flour

1 tsp baking powder
1 tsp vanilla
1 can cherry pie filling
2 tsp sugar, for topping

Cream butter or margarine and sugar together until fluffy. Add eggs and beat well. Add dry ingredients and vanilla. Using floured fingertips, spread half of this batter in a greased 9"x13" baking pan. Spread pie filling over entire surface of dough. Drop remaining batter in dollops over pie filling. Sprinkle with 2 teaspoons sugar. Bake at 350° for 30 to 35 minutes. Cool. Cut into squares.

Hint: You can use other pie fillings such as blueberry, lemon, pineapple, strawberry, etc. to suit your taste and color scheme. This was one of the most requested recipes from my TV segments!

153

RAPE CAKE

2½ C confectioners' sugar
1¾ C flour
4 eggs
1 tsp vanilla

3½ to 4 C green and/or red seedless grapes
Confectioners' sugar, for sprinkling on top

Beat eggs and confectioners' sugar until fluffy. Add flour and vanilla. Pour into a well greased 9-inch springform pan or 9"x13" pan. Sprinkle with grapes until top of cake is completely covered. Bake at 350° until golden. Springform cake takes 50 to 55 minutes. Oblong takes 30 to 40 minutes. Cool and sprinkle with confectioners' sugar. Garnish with frosted grapes if desired.

FROSTED GRAPES:

Egg white
Granulated sugar

Small clusters of grapes

Beat egg white with a fork. Dip grape clusters into egg white and then into sugar. Dry on a wire rack.

Hint: This is an old German recipe that my grandmother used to make. It has an unusual texture and flavor and is great to make when grapes are in season or for special occasions. It freezes well. Frosted grapes are a pretty garnish that can be used any time.

ATE NUT CHOCOLATE CHIP CAKE

8 oz chopped dates
1 C boiling water
½ tsp vanilla
1 tsp baking soda
1 C butter or margarine
1 C sugar

2 eggs
1¾ C flour
2 tsp cocoa
½ tsp salt
6 oz chocolate chips
1 C walnuts, coarsely chopped

Combine dates, boiling water, vanilla and baking soda. Set aside. Cream sugar with butter or margarine until fluffy. Add eggs. Add dry ingredients alternately with liquid from date mixture. Add dates and any remaining liquid at end. Top with chocolate chips and walnuts. Bake in a greased 9"x13" pan at 350° for 35 minutes, or until toothpick, inserted in center, comes out clean.

Hint: This is a delicious moist cake. Even if you don't like dates, you'll love it!

PUMPKIN POUND CAKE

1 C brown sugar
1 C granulated sugar
1 C butter or margarine
4 eggs
16 oz can pumpkin or 2 C fresh
  pureed pumpkin
3 C flour
½ tsp salt
2 tsp baking soda

1 T cinnamon
1 tsp nutmeg
½ tsp allspice
½ tsp ginger
½ C pecans, chopped
½ C raisins
Confectioners' sugar, for
  sprinkling on top

Combine butter or margarine and both sugars and beat until fluffy. Add eggs and beat for about 2 minutes. Add pumpkin and mix well. Sift together flour, baking soda and spices and add to pumpkin mixture. Beat for 2 more minutes. Stir in pecans and raisins. Pour into a greased and floured 10-inch tube pan. Bake at 350° for 60 to 65 minutes or until toothpick, inserted in center, comes out clean. Cool 15 minutes and then remove from pan to a wire rack. Sprinkle with confectioners' sugar or frost with Cream Cheese Frosting.

CREAM CHEESE FROSTING:

3 oz cream cheese, softened
¼ C margarine, softened
1 tsp vanilla

3 C confectioners', sugar
5 to 6 T milk
Pecan, for garnish

Beat cream cheese and margarine together. Add vanilla, confectioners' sugar and enough milk to make a spreadable consistency. Garnish with pecan halves or chopped pecans.

Hint: This cake has a wonderful texture and flavor. It is a great way to use fresh pureed pumpkin. The cake freezes well, even if frosted.

CHOCOLATE ZUCCHINI CAKE

¾ C butter or margarine
2 C sugar
3 eggs
1½ tsp vanilla
2 C zucchini, coarsely grated
½ C sour milk or plain yogurt
2½ C flour
1 tsp salt

½ C cocoa
2½ tsp baking powder
1½ tsp baking soda
½ tsp cinnamon
½ tsp allspice
Confectioners's sugar, for
  sprinkling on top

Cream butter or margarine and sugar until fluffy. Add eggs, one at a time and beat well. Add vanilla. Then add grated zucchini and sour milk or yogurt. Sift dry ingredients together and then add to creamed mixture. Grease and flour a 10-inch bundt or tube pan. Pour in batter and bake at 350° for 45 to 55 minutes or until toothpick, inserted in center, comes out clean. Cool in pan. Sprinkle with confectioners' sugar.

Hint: This is a dense and moist chocolate cake that does not taste of zucchini. It freezes well and is a great recipe to make when you have extra zucchini in your garden. A food processor makes grating the zucchini a cinch! You can also bake this in a 9"x13" pan at 350° for 25 to 30 minutes.

CHOCOLATE CHIP CAKE

1 stick butter or margarine, softened
1 C sugar
2 eggs
1 C sour cream or yogurt
1 tsp vanilla

2 C flour
1 tsp baking soda
1 tsp baking powder
1 C chocolate chips

Cream butter or margarine with sugar until fluffy. Add eggs, sour cream and vanilla. Fold in remaining ingredients. Pour into a greased and floured 9-inch springform pan.

TOPPING:

3 T butter or margarine, melted
4 T sugar

1 tsp cinnamon

Melt butter or margarine. Fold in sugar and cinnamon. Spread this mixture over batter in pan. Bake at 350° for 50 to 55 minutes, or until toothpick, inserted in center, comes out clean.

Hint: This is a moist cake that is perfect for brunch or anytime. It freezes well.

CHOCOLATE INTRIGUE CAKE

3 C flour
2 tsp baking powder
½ tsp salt
⅓ lb (1⅓ sticks) butter
   or margarine
2 C sugar
3 eggs
1 C milk
1½ tsp vanilla
¾ C chocolate syrup (Hershey's)
¼ tsp baking soda
¼ tsp mint extract
Confectioners' sugar, for
   sprinkling on top

Sift together flour, baking powder and salt and set aside. Cream butter or margarine and sugar until fluffy. Add eggs, one at a time, beating well after each. Combine milk and vanilla and add alternately with flour mixture. Pour two-thirds of that batter into a 10-inch greased and floured tube or bundt pan. Combine chocolate syrup, baking soda and mint and add to the remaining dough. Spoon this chocolate batter over white batter, trying not to mix them. Bake at 350° for 45 to 55 minutes, or until toothpick, inserted in center, comes out clean. Cool. Remove from pan and sprinkle with confectioners' sugar.

Hint: This cake is a family favorite. It is the birthday cake my sons most often request! In fact, one year I mailed it to one of my sons at college for his birthday. It arrived in one piece and still tasted fresh after four days in a carton! It freezes beautifully, although we seldom have any leftovers to freeze.

CHOCOLATE PEANUT BUTTER PIZZA COOKIE

½ C granulated sugar
½ C brown sugar, firmly packed
1 stick butter or margarine, softened
½ C peanut butter
½ tsp vanilla
1 egg
1½ C flour
2 C mini-marshmallows
1 C chocolate chips

Cream butter or margarine and both sugars until fluffy. Add peanut butter, egg and vanilla. Mix well and fold in flour. Fold in flour. Mix well and pat onto a greased 12 to 14-inch pizza pan, forming a ridge of dough around the edge of the pan. Bake at 375° for 12 minutes or until golden. Remove from oven and sprinkle with mini-marshmallows and chocolate chips. Bake an additional 5 to 6 minutes. Cool and cut into wedges.

Hint: The name of this recipe doesn't usually appeal to people unless you describe it to them. Once they see it or taste it they'll flip! It tastes best when made several hours, or even a day in advance, of serving.

CHOCOLATE SYRUP CAKE

1 stick butter or margarine
1 C sugar
4 eggs
1¼ C flour
¾ tsp baking soda

16 oz chocolate syrup
1 tsp vanilla
Confectioners' sugar, for
   sprinkling on top (optional)

Cream butter or margarine and sugar until fluffy. Add eggs, one at a time, beating after each addition. Combine flour and baking soda and add alternately with chocolate syrup. Add vanilla. Pour into a greased 9"x13" pan. Bake at 350° for 35 to 40 minutes, or until toothpick, inserted in center, comes out clean. Sprinkle with confectioners' sugar or frost with Coffee Frosting or your own favorite frosting.

COFFEE FROSTING:

4 T butter or margarine
2 to 2½ C confectioners' sugar,
   sifted
1 tsp vanilla

3 to 4 T hot strong coffee
   (1 tsp instant coffee mixed
   with 3 to 4 T water)

Cream butter or margarine and sugar until fluffy. Add confectioners' sugar, coffee and vanilla. Mix until smooth. Spread on cake. If desired, decorate with walnut halves or chocolate chips.

Hint: This is one of the easiest and tastiest chocolate cakes to make. I always keep a can of Hershey syrup on hand in case I need a cake in an emergency. It's delicious even without frosting and perfect to bring to a picnic or barbecue.

KAHLUA BROWNIE HEART

2 squares unsweetened chocolate
1 stick butter or margarine
2 eggs
1 C sugar
1 tsp baking powder
½ tsp instant coffee
   powder or crystals

1 C flour
3 T coffee liqueur (Kahlua)
Confectioners' sugar for
   sprinkling on top (optional)
Whipped cream, for garnish
Raspberries or strawberries,
   for garnish

Melt chocolate and butter or margarine over a double boiler or in a microwave on medium power for 2 to 2½ minutes. Whisk in eggs. Beat in remaining ingredients. Pour into a greased and floured 9-inch heart-shaped pan. Bake at 350° for approximately 18 to 20 minutes or until toothpick, inserted in center, comes out clean. Do not overbake; cake should be fudgey and moist. Cool on wire rack and turn out onto a platter. Sprinkle with confectioners' sugar and decorate border with whipped cream. Garnish cream with fresh raspberries or strawberries.

Hint: *If you are making this for Valentine's Day garnish with heart-shaped candies. You can also make this recipe as Kahlua Brownies in a 9-inch square pan.*

SOUR CREAM POUND CAKE

1 stick butter or margarine
2 C sugar
4 eggs
1 tsp extract (vanilla, lemon,
   orange or almond)
1 tsp baking powder
½ tsp baking soda

¼ tsp salt
3 C flour
1 C sour cream
1 C chopped nuts, raisins or
   chocolate chips (optional)
Confectioners' sugar, for
   sprinkling on top

Cream butter or margarine and sugar until fluffy. Add eggs and mix well. Add dry ingredients alternately with sour cream. Add extract and any desired optional ingredients. Pour into a greased 10-inch tube pan and bake at 350° for 50 to 60 minutes. This may also be baked in two 9"x5" loaf pans or four mini-loaf pans for about 25 to 30 minutes. Sift with confectioners' sugar or frost with Lemon Glaze.

LEMON GLAZE:

1 C confectioners' sugar
Whisk together and frost cake.

2 T lemon juice

Hint: *You can make several different cakes by varying the extracts and optional ingredients. Examples of combinations are: vanilla extract and chocolate chips, almond extract and chopped almonds, orange or lemon extract and raisins, etc.*

159

Mom's Jellyroll

4 eggs
¾ C sugar, divided
½ tsp vanilla

¾ C flour, sifted
1 tsp baking powder

Separate eggs. In the small bowl of an electric mixer, beat egg whites until stiff, but not dry. Add half of the sugar to this and beat just until it is incorporated. Set aside. In the large bowl of the mixer, beat egg yolks with remaining sugar for 7 to 10 minutes, or until mixture becomes thick and lemon-colored. Add vanilla. Combine flour and baking powder and add at low speed to yolk mixture, alternately with egg whites. Fold just until blended. Do not overbeat. Pour batter into a 15½"x10½"x1" jellyroll pan, that has been greased and lined with wax paper or parchment paper that has also been well greased. Bake at 375° for 10 to 12 minutes, or until golden. Immediately turn cake out onto a dish towel that has been well sprinkled with confectioners' sugar. Peel off wax paper. Place another piece of wax paper on top of cake roll and roll up starting at long edge, using towel as an aide. Place cake, (still in towel) seam side down, on a wire rack to cool. When cool, fill with one of the following fillings:

FILLINGS:

Jam

12 oz jam or jelly of your choice

Beat jam or jelly with fork. Unroll cake roll, remove wax paper and spread with jam. Roll up and sprinkle roll with confectioners' sugar.

Pineapple Cream

20 oz can crushed pineapple, well drained

1 pt whipping cream, whipped

Whip cream until it has a spreadable consistency. Mix with drained pineapple. Unroll cake roll, remove wax paper and spread with half of the pineapple mixture. Roll up. Cut off a diagonal slice on each end of the cake and frost entire outside of cake roll with remaining pineapple mixture. Refrigerate until serving time.

Strawberry Cream
1 pt strawberries
2 T sugar

1 pt whipping cream, divided
Vanilla sugar*, to taste

Wash, hull and slice all the berries, setting aside the six or seven nicest looking ones. Add the sugar to the sliced berries and allow them to set for awhile, until a little juice forms. Unroll the cake roll, remove the wax paper and drizzle the strawberry juice over the cake roll. Whip all the cream. Fold the sliced berries into half of the whipped cream. Spread this over the cake and roll it up. Cut off a diagonal slice on each end of the roll. Frost outside of cake roll with plain whipped cream, to which you have added vanilla sugar*, to taste. Garnish with reserved whole berries. Refrigerate until serving time.

Hint: This recipe was my mother's old standby whenever she had unexpected guests, for she always had four eggs, a little flour, sugar and jam in the house! Mom says, "currant jelly or apricot jam are my favorites". When she wanted a spectacular looking and tasting dessert and strawberries weren't in season, she made it with the pineapple filling. During strawberry season, she always used strawberries. Don't be discouraged by the length of the recipe. Reading the directions takes longer than it does to prepare it. The jellyroll may be made a day in advance by covering it with plastic wrap. Frost a few hours before serving.

*Vanilla sugar is made by placing a vanilla bean in a jar of granulated sugar and leaving it there for a few days or up to several months, while it imparts its essence and flavors the sugar. Vanilla sugar is often used to flavor whipped cream, or it can be used in cake or cookie recipes that call for both sugar and vanilla.

CHOCOLATE ROLL (BUCHE DE NOEL)

6 eggs
¾ C sugar, divided
⅓ C unsweetened cocoa

1 tsp vanilla extract
½ tsp almond extract
Confectioners' sugar

Separate eggs and place yolks into small bowl and whites into large bowl of electric mixer. Let egg whites warm to room temperature, about 1 hour. Grease bottom and sides of a 10½"x15½"x1" jellyroll pan, then line with wax paper. Grease wax paper also. At high speed, beat egg whites just until soft peaks form when beater is slowly raised. Gradually beat in ¼ cup sugar, beating until stiff peaks form. In a small bowl, with same beater, at high speed, beat egg yolks and ½ cup sugar until thick and lemon-colored; about 5 minutes. At low speed, beat in cocoa and extracts, until combined. With a rubber spatula, using an under and over motion, gently fold yolk mixture into egg whites, until combined. Turn into prepared jellyroll pan, spreading evenly. Bake at 375° for 12 to 14 minutes, or until surface springs back when gently pressed with fingertip. While cake is baking, sift confectioners' sugar onto a clean dish towel. When cake comes out of oven, immediately turn it over onto towel. Gently peel off wax paper. With a very sharp knife, trim edges. Starting with long edge, roll up cake in towel, jellyroll fashion. (Cake tends to crack slightly when rolled.) Place seam side down, on wire rack, for 30 minutes, or until cool. Meanwhile, make Mocha Cream Filling. To fill, gently unroll cake; remove towel. Spread cake with filling; roll up again. Cut off a diagonal slice on each end of the cake. Place seam side down, on serving platter. Refrigerate 1 hour, or until serving time. To serve, slice on diagonal with serrated knife.

MOCHA CREAM FILLING:

1 C whipping cream
¼ C confectioners' sugar, sifted
2 T unsweetened cocoa

1½ tsp instant coffee
1 tsp vanilla extract

Combine all ingredients in medium bowl. Refrigerate, along with beater blades, until well chilled; at least 40 minutes. Beat filling mixture until stiff. Spread over cake roll, reserving a small amount of filling. Roll up and sprinkle with confectioners' sugar. I usually reserve a small amount of the mocha whipped cream so that I have enough to make rosettes of cream as a decoration on the outside of the chocolate roll. I usually place a chocolate chip, strawberry, raspberry or candied cherry on each rosette.

Hint: This chocolate roll is an ecumenical recipe, for it can serve as a Buche de Noel at Christmas, or since it contains no flour, as a Chocolate Roll for Passover.

CHOCOLATE ALMOND CHEESECAKE

CRUST:

1½ C chocolate cookie crumbs
1 C blanched almonds, toasted and chopped

⅓ C sugar
6 T butter or margarine, softened

Combine all ingredients and pat onto bottom and up sides of a 9-inch springform pan.

FILLING:

1½ lbs cream cheese, softened
1 C sugar
4 eggs

⅓ C heavy cream
¼ C almond liqueur (Amaretto)
1 tsp vanilla

In a large bowl, combine cream cheese and sugar and beat until fluffy. Add eggs, one at a time, beating well after each addition. Add cream, almond liqueur and vanilla and beat until light and fluffy. Pour over crust in springform pan and bake at 375° for 30 minutes. Transfer to a cake rack and allow to stand for 5 minutes (cake will not be set).

TOPPING:

2 C sour cream
1 T sugar

1 tsp vanilla
Slivered almonds, toasted

Combine these ingredients and spread evenly on the cake and bake for an additional 5 minutes. Transfer to a rack. Allow cake to cool completely and then refrigerate it, lightly covered, overnight. To garnish, place slivered toasted almonds around top outer edge of cake.

Hint: Any kind of plain chocolate cookies may be used to make the crumbs for the crust. You can grind the cookies and almonds in the food processor, using the steel blade, and then add the butter or margarine and sugar.

GRAHAM CRACKER PIE CRUST

1¼ C graham cracker crumbs
¼ C sugar

⅓ C butter or margarine, melted

Combine all ingredients and pat into a 9-inch pie plate or springform pan.

Hint: This is a very easy pie crust recipe that goes well with almost any dessert filling. There is no need to buy the crumbs; it's more economical to crush the graham crackers in your blender or processor. You can substitute chocolate cookies to make a Chocolate Pie Crust.

163

FLAKY FOOD PROCESSOR PIE CRUST

1 C and 1 T flour   ½ T vinegar
½ C frozen butter or margarine,   ¼ C ginger ale or club soda
cut into chunks

With steel blade of food processor, mix flour and butter or margarine with on/off turns until mixture resembles coarse oatmeal. Combine ginger ale with vinegar and add through feed tube while machine is running. Process just until dough forms a ball around blade. Remove from machine and wrap in plastic wrap. Chill in refrigerator for at least an hour before rolling out.

Yield: One 9-inch or 10-inch crust

Hint: For a 2-crust pie, double the recipe. This is a flaky pie crust that is easy to roll out. It is delicious with either a sweet or savory filling. The ball of dough may be kept in the freezer for several weeks or even months and taken out when needed. Defrost just enough to roll out.

GRASSHOPPER PIE

CRUST:

1½ C chocolate cookie crumbs   ½ C melted butter or margarine

Crush cookies in a food processor or blender and add melted butter or margarine. Pat into 9-inch pie plate. Bake at 350° for 10 minutes.

FILLING:

32 large marshmallows
¼ C creme de menthe   1½ C whipping cream
3 T creme de cocoa   Few drops green food coloring

Melt marshmallows in double boiler or in microwave. Add liqueurs and cool. Whip cream and fold into marshmallow mixture. Add food coloring. Pour into cooled chocolate pie crust. Refrigerate for several hours before serving.

Hint: Any kind of plain chocolate cookies may be used for the crust. This is a light and refreshing dessert.

LEMON CHIFFON PIE

1 pkg unflavored gelatin
¼ C cold water
4 eggs, separated
1 C sugar, divided

½ C fresh lemon juice
1 tsp lemon rind, grated
Pinch salt
Pie crust (pg. 164), baked and cooled

Soften gelatin in water. Beat egg yolks, lemon juice, salt and ½ cup of the sugar. Cook in a double boiler or over boiling water until it reaches a thick custardy consistency. Add softened gelatin and rind. Stir well. Cool. Beat egg whites until soft peaks form. Add remaining ½ cup sugar and beat until stiff, but not dry. Fold whites into lemon mixture. Pour into a 9-inch pie crust that has been baked until golden. Refrigerate until serving time.

Hint: To get pie crust golden, prick all over with a fork and bake at 425° for 10 to 15 minutes. This is a light dessert that slides down easily after a big meal. You can substitute limes for the lemon and have Lime Chiffon Pie.

STRAWBERRY CHEESE PIE

Graham Cracker Pie Crust (pg. 163)
1 lb cream cheese, at room temp.
2 eggs
⅔ C sugar
1 tsp vanilla

1½ C sour cream
2 T sugar
¾ to 1 C red currant jelly
2 pts fresh strawberries

Combine cream cheese, eggs and ⅔ cup sugar and beat for about 10 minutes. Fold in vanilla. Pour into prepared crust and bake at 325° for 40 to 45 minutes. Mix sour cream with 2 tablespoons sugar, spoon on top of pie and bake 5 minutes longer. Cool. Melt jelly until syrupy. Coat each strawberry with jelly and place on pie, stem end down. Pour remaining jelly over the top. Chill. When fresh berries are not available, canned pie filling may be used as topping.

Hint: You can substitute a store-bought crust if you do not want to make your own. Also, blueberries may be substituted for the strawberries. This makes a gorgeous dessert that takes little time or skill but looks as if you're an expert! You can also use this recipe to make 12 muffin-sized Strawberry Cheese Tarts.

ECAN PIE

9" pie shell, partially baked
½ C butter or margarine
1¼ C sugar
½ C light corn syrup

3 eggs, slightly beaten
1 tsp vanilla
1½ C pecans
Whipped cream, for garnish

Prepare partially baked pie shell using your favorite single pie crust. Bake 3 to 4 minutes. Cook butter or margarine, sugar and corn syrup over low heat until butter or margarine melts. Do not let mixture boil. Cool slightly. Stir in eggs and mix well. Add vanilla and pecans. Pour filling into the pie crust. Bake at 375° for 40 to 45 minutes. Pie should be soft in center when removed from oven. If desired, garnish with whipped cream or serve with vanilla ice cream.

Hint: This is one of the simplest, yet most delicious pecan pies I've ever tasted. It freezes well. Use the Flaky Processor Pie Crust (pg. 164) or your own favorite pie crust. Corn syrup is the same as Karo syrup and is found in the baking section in supermarkets.

RUIT SALAD PIE

Graham Cracker Pie Crust (pg.163)
Large can (approx. 29 oz) fruit cocktail

1 pt sour cream
1 tsp vanilla
¼ C sugar

Drain fruit cocktail well. Combine sour cream, sugar and vanilla. Add drained fruit to this mixture. Pour into a 9-inch unbaked Graham Cracker Pie Crust (pg. 163). Bake at 350° for 20 minutes or until mixture is set. Cool and chill for several hours before serving.

Hint: A prepared graham cracker crust may be purchased if you want to save time. For a large crowd, this recipe may be doubled, baked in a 9"x13" pan, and cut into squares which may be placed in paper baking cups.

Cookies and Pastries

CHOCOLATE MINT BROWNIES

¼ lb butter or margarine
1 C sugar
1 tsp vanilla
2 eggs

2 oz unsweetened baking chocolate, melted
½ C flour
5 to 6 oz mint chocolate chips

Cream butter or margarine and sugar until fluffy. Add vanilla, eggs and melted chocolate. Fold in flour and mint chocolate chips. Bake in a greased 8- or 9-inch square pan at 325° for 23 to 25 minutes, or until toothpick, inserted in center, comes out clean.

Hint: People are pleasantly surprised when they bite into these because they look like ordinary brownies but they have a delicious minty flavor!

MICROWAVE BROWNIES

1 stick butter or margarine
1 C sugar
1 egg

1 tsp vanilla
½ C unsweetened cocoa
½ C flour

Cream butter or margarine and sugar until fluffy. Add egg and vanilla and mix well. Fold in cocoa and flour until blended. Pour into a greased 9-inch pie plate. Cook on high for 4½ minutes, turning once or twice. Cool on wire rack.

Hint: On the whole, I haven't been pleased with the quality and taste of baked from scratch recipes in the microwave. However, this is an exception! These brownies have a nice texture and a delicious taste. If you use an egg substitute, the only fat will be from the margarine, since cocoa contains no butterfat.

FROSTED MINT BROWNIES

½ C butter or margarine
1 C sugar
2 eggs
½ C flour
⅛ tsp salt

⅛ tsp baking powder
2 squares unsweetened baking
   chocolate, melted
½ tsp vanilla
½ C walnuts, chopped (optional)

Cream butter or margarine and sugar until well blended. Add eggs and beat until fluffy. Beat in baking chocolate. At low speed of mixer, add flour, salt and baking powder. Add vanilla and nuts, if desired. Bake in a greased 8 or 9-inch square pan at 350° for 25 minutes, or until done. Do not overbake or brownies will get dry. (If not frosting these brownies, cut while warm. If frosting them, do not cut.)

MINT FROSTING:

1 C confectioners' sugar, sifted
1 to 2 T milk
2 T butter or margarine, softened

¼ tsp mint extract
1 to 2 drops green food coloring

Cream confectioners' sugar and butter or margarine. Add mint, green color and 1 tablespoon milk. Beat, adding milk until frosting is of spreading consistency. Spread this mixture over cooled brownies.

CHOCOLATE SHADOW:

1 T unsweetened baking chocolate
1 T butter or margarine

When the frosting is set, melt this remaining chocolate and butter or margarine together. Spread evenly over green frosting. Place in refrigerator and chill until Chocolate Shadow is firm. Cut into squares. These freeze well.

Hint: This is a delicious brownie recipe, even without the frosting. When frosted, these are beautiful, especially on a tray of assorted cookies and pastries at the holidays. However, you can change the color of the frosting to suit an occasion or fit a color scheme. For instance, pink or light blue can be used for a baby shower. I usually double this recipe and bake it in a 9"x13" pan for only a few minutes longer than in the 8 or 9-inch pan.

RASPBERRY BROWNIES

2 oz unsweetened chocolate
1 stick butter or margarine
2 eggs
⅔ C sugar
½ C seedless raspberry jam
2 tsp raspberry liqueur (Chambord, or Framboise (optional)
⅔ C flour
¼ tsp salt, or to taste
½ tsp baking powder
⅓ C chocolate chips
Confectioners' sugar, for sprinkling on the top

In a double boiler, melt unsweetened chocolate and butter or margarine, stirring until smooth; cool slightly. Whisk in eggs, sugar, jam and liqueur. Fold in flour, salt, baking powder and chocolate chips. The mixture will be thin. Pour into a greased, 8 or 9-inch square pan. Bake at 350° for 25 to 30 minutes or until a toothpick, inserted in the center, comes out clean. Cool on a wire rack. Cut when cool.

Hint: You can melt the butter or margarine and chocolate in a microwave instead of a double boiler. To serve, sprinkle confectioners' sugar on the brownies or, to make them look spectacular, cut them into small squares and make a rosette of whipped cream in the center of each square. Place a fresh raspberry on each rosette. Serve on a platter lined with a white doily. The brownies may be made up to 2 days in advance or frozen. Decorate with whipped cream and berries 1 hour in advance.

ERY RICH CREAM CHEESE BROWNIES

1 C butter or margarine	2 C sugar
4 squares unsweetened baking chocolate	1 C walnuts, coarsely chopped
4 eggs, divided	½ tsp vanilla
1 C flour	8 oz cream cheese, softened
½ tsp salt	½ C sugar

Melt butter or margarine and chocolate in a double boiler over low heat. Whisk in 2 cups sugar and three of the eggs until well blended. With a wooden spoon, stir in flour, salt, nuts and vanilla. Spread evenly in a greased 9"x13" pan. In a small bowl with an electric mixer, beat cream cheese, remaining egg and ½ cup sugar. Beat for 2 minutes, or until light and fluffy. With a large spoon, drop dollops of cream cheese mixture over brownie batter. Using a knife, lightly near the top surface of brownies, make a criss-cross pattern through cream cheese dollops. Bake at 350° for 35 to 40 minutes, or until toothpick, inserted in center, comes out clean. Cool before cutting.

Hint: These are very rich, so cut into small squares. They freeze well and are a nice addition to a pastry platter at the holidays or for large parties.

LACK BOTTOMS OR CHOCOLATE CREAM CHEESE CUPCAKES

1 C water	1 tsp baking soda
½ C canola oil	½ tsp salt
1 T vinegar	8 oz cream cheese, softened
1 tsp vanilla	1 egg
1½ C flour	½ C sugar
1 C sugar	6 oz chocolate chips
¼ C cocoa	

Combine first four ingredients. Then add flour, sugar, cocoa, baking soda and salt. Place this mixture in two muffin or cupcake pans lined with baking papers. Then, using an electric mixer, mix cream cheese, egg and sugar until light and fluffy. Add chocolate chips. Place a teaspoon of this mixture on top of each cupcake. Bake at 350° for 15 to 20 minutes or until toothpick, inserted in center, comes out clean.

Yield: 2 dozen cupcakes

Hint: I often make these in mini-cupcake tins, using mini-chocolate chips. The recipe yields at least 3 dozen mini-cupcakes. These freeze well and look pretty on a platter of cookies and pastries.

CHOCOLATE MACAROONS

2 oz semi-sweet chocolate
2 T butter or margarine
⅓ C sugar

2 eggs, lightly beaten
1 tsp vanilla
2⅔ C (7 oz pkg) coconut

Melt chocolate and butter or margarine in a double boiler over low heat. Stir until smooth. Remove from heat and blend in sugar, eggs and vanilla. Beat well. Stir in coconut. Drop by teaspoon onto greased, or parchment-lined, cookie sheets leaving 1½ inches between each. Bake at 350° for 12 to 15 minutes. Cool on wire rack.

Yield: 3 dozen macaroons

Hint: These are quick to make and quick to disappear!

DANISH HAZELNUT COOKIES

¾ C hazelnuts (filberts)
¾ C flour

1 stick unsalted butter
¾ C confectioners' sugar

Grind hazelnuts finely in food processor using steel blade. Add flour and sugar. Mix well. Cut butter into chunks and add to processor. Pulse motor just until dough is blended and forms a ball on blade. Remove and shape dough into two long rolls the diameter of a quarter. Wrap each roll in plastic wrap and place in refrigerator for at least one hour or in freezer for up to three months. To bake, remove from refrigerator or freezer and cut into slices ⅓-inch thick. Place on greased cookie sheets. Do not place too closely together because they expand. Bake at 350° for 10 to 12 minutes. Sprinkle with confectioners' sugar as soon as they come out of the oven. These will keep in a tin at room temperature for several weeks or may be frozen for several months.

Hint: If you don't have a food processor, you can chop the nuts in a blender or by hand. Then use a mixer to make the dough. These cookies have a very delicate flavor. They are like homemade Icebox Cookies because you can keep the dough in the refrigerator and slice and bake them as needed.

$\mathcal{S}$ LICED BUTTER COOKIES

½ lb butter, softened	2¼ C flour
¾ C sugar	1 tsp vanilla
1 egg yolk	

Cream butter and sugar until fluffy. Add remaining ingredients. Roll into logs about 1½ inches in diameter. Wrap in plastic wrap and chill for at least 1 hour, or up to a few days. Slice ¼-inch thick onto greased cookie sheets. Bake at 400° for about 10 to 12 minutes, or until golden on edges.

Hint: *I usually use half butter and half margarine in this recipe. These are like homemade Icebox Cookies, because you can keep the dough in the refrigerator and slice and bake them as needed. You can also freeze the logs of dough for up to 2 months and remove them from the freezer and slice, as needed. Once baked, these cookies keep well in a tin at room temperature for at least a week, or in the freezer for a couple of months.*

$\mathcal{A}$ LASKA LOGS

¾ C flour, sifted	¼ tsp salt
1 tsp baking powder	3 eggs, well beaten
1 C sugar	1 C dates, chopped
1 C almonds or walnuts, chopped	Granulated sugar, for topping

Sift dry ingredients together and stir in remaining ingredients. Pour into a greased 9"x13" pan and bake at 325° for 30 to 40 minutes. Cut at once into 2-inch bars and roll in granulated sugar while still warm.

Hint: *These make a nice addition to a holiday pastry tray.*

PAINTBRUSH COOKIES

1½ C confectioners' sugar
1 C butter or margarine, softened
1 egg
1 tsp vanilla
½ tsp almond extract

2½ C flour
1 tsp baking soda
1 tsp cream of tartar
Egg Yolk Paint

Combine confectioners' sugar, butter or margarine, egg, vanilla and almond extract. Stir in flour, baking soda and cream of tartar. Cover and refrigerate for 2 to 3 hours or overnight. When ready to roll out, divide dough in half. Roll each half ¼inch thick on a lightly floured surface. Cut into desired shapes with cookie cutters. Place on a lightly greased cookie sheet. Prepare Egg Yolk Paint. Paint designs on cookies with small paintbrushes. Bake at 375° until edges are light brown, 7 to 8 minutes.

Yield: About 5 dozen 2 to 2½-inch cookies

EGG YOLK PAINT:

Mix 1 egg yolk and ¼ teaspoon water. Divide mixture among several small custard cups. Tint each with different food color to make bright colors. If paint thickens while standing, stir in a few drops water.

Hint: This dough is easy to roll and not nearly as messy as the usual cutout cookie dough. This is a great project to do with children or grandchildren, especially at the holiday season. Not only do the children like cutting out the cookie shapes, they love painting on them, too!

ANN HAGLE COOKIES

1 C butter or margarine, softened
1 C sugar
1 egg, separated
2 C flour

1 tsp cinnamon
1 T water
2¼ oz (1 small pkg) almonds, sliced

Beat butter or margarine and sugar until fluffy. Add egg yolk and mix well. Add flour and cinnamon and blend well. Press lightly into a greased 10½"x15½"x1" jellyroll pan. Beat egg white with water and brush over the dough. Sprinkle with almonds. Bake at 350° for 20 to 25 minutes, or until golden. Cut immediately into 1½ to 2-inch squares.

Hint: I use a stick of butter and a stick of margarine. These are great cookies to make when you're in a hurry, since it is easier cutting squares than making drop cookies. These keep well in a tin for a few weeks or they may be frozen.

LEMON SQUARES

1 C flour
½ C butter or margarine, softened
¼ C confectioners' sugar
1 C granulated sugar
2 eggs
2 tsp lemon rind, grated

2 T fresh lemon juice
½ tsp baking powder
¼ tsp salt
Confectioners' sugar, for
sprinkling on top

Cream flour, butter or margarine and confectioners' sugar until fluffy. Press into ungreased 8-inch square baking pan, building up ½-inch edges. Bake at 350° for 20 minutes. Beat granulated sugar, eggs, lemon rind, lemon juice, baking powder and salt until light and fluffy, about 3 minutes. Pour over baked layer. Bake at 350° for about 25 minutes more, or just until no indentation remains when touched in center. Cool and sprinkle with confectioners' sugar. Cut into 1-inch squares.

Hint: These may be frozen for several weeks or kept in a tin for several days. They are wonderful to serve with afternoon tea or coffee, and also are a nice addition to a tray of assorted pastries.

LEMON MERINGUE COOKIES

3 egg whites
½ tsp cream of tartar
1 C sugar

1 T lemon rind, grated
Nonstick cooking spray

Beat egg whites until foamy and add cream of tartar. Gradually beat in sugar, 2 tablespoons at a time, until stiff glossy peaks form. Fold in lemon rind. Drop by teaspoon onto baking sheets that have been sprayed with nonstick cooking spray. Bake at 275° for 20 to 25 minutes. Cool on wire rack.

Yield: 5 to 6 dozen

Hint: These delicious cookies have no fat or cholesterol and contain approximately 35 calories each. The lemon imparts a wonderful flavor. These make a wonderful gift for someone who is on a very restricted low fat or fat free diet. To achieve maximum volume from the egg whites, they should be at room temperature when beaten.

WHOOPIE PIES

2 C flour
1 tsp baking soda
¼ tsp salt
1 C sugar
⅓ C cocoa

⅓ C canola oil
1 egg
1 tsp vanilla
¾ C milk

Combine flour, baking soda, salt, sugar and cocoa. Add remaining ingredients and beat well. Drop by tablespoon onto greased cookie sheet, leaving room for spreading; six fit on each cookie sheet. Bake at 350° for 8 to 10 minutes, or until cake tester comes out clean. Cool before filling. These may be frozen.

FILLING:

1 C confectioners' sugar
3 heaping T marshmallow fluff

1 stick butter or margarine, softened
1 tsp vanilla

Combine all ingredients and blend until fluffy. Spread some filling on each large cookie. Top with another cookie to form a Whoopie Pie. Sprinkle with confectioners' sugar.

Yield: 10 to 12 whoopie pies

Hint: These are delicious and fun to make with children. Over the years I have made them with one of my son's nursery school classes, with another son's Cub Scout pack and for another son's birthday party.

176

RUGELACH

DOUGH:

½ lb butter or margarine, softened   1½ C flour

½ lb cottage cheese (small curd)

Cream together butter or margarine and cottage cheese until smooth. Add flour and mix until dough is formed. Chill for several hours or overnight. Remove from refrigerator and divide into quarters. Roll out each quarter into a circle and cut into 10 to 12 small triangular wedges. Place a spoonful of desired filling on each wedge and roll up. Bake at 350° on ungreased cookie sheets for 20 to 25 minutes or until golden.

CINNAMON SUGAR FILLING:

¾ C sugar   ¾ C walnuts, finely chopped

1 tsp cinnamon

Combine all ingredients. If using this filling, sprinkle each triangle with extra sugar and cinnamon before baking.

CHOCOLATE CHIP FILLING:

½ C brown sugar, lightly packed   4 T mini-chocolate chips

1 tsp cinnamon   Confectioners' sugar, for

¼ C walnuts, finely chopped   sprinkling on top

2 T cocoa

Combine all ingredients. If using this filling, sprinkle each triangle with confectioners' sugar after baking.

Hint: I usually use half butter and half margarine in the dough. Dough may be made in the food processor using the steel blade or with a mixer.

APRICOT STRUDEL

DOUGH:

2 sticks butter or margarine   2 C flour
1 C sour cream

Soften butter or margarine and mix with sour cream. Add flour and beat until well mixed. Roll into a ball and wrap in plastic wrap. Refrigerate for several hours or overnight.

FILLING:

10 vanilla wafers, finely chopped   12 oz apricot jam
1 C walnuts, chopped

Finely crush vanilla wafers and walnuts in food processor or with a nut chopper, being careful not to chop too finely. Fold in jam.

STRUDEL:

Remove dough from refrigerator and cut into four pieces. Roll out one piece at a time, leaving the remaining ones in the refrigerator. Roll into a rectangle about 7"x11" and spread surface with a quarter of the filling mixture to within 1 inch of the outside edges of dough. Roll up jellyroll fashion, sealing edges with water. Place rolls, seam side down, two to a sheet, on an ungreased cookie sheet. Bake at 425° for 10 minutes. Then reduce temperature to 350° and bake for 20 minutes or until golden. While still warm, slice into 1-inch pieces. When cool, sprinkle with confectioners' sugar.

Yield: about 5 dozen pieces

Hint: *I use a stick of butter and a stick of margarine for this dough. This strudel keeps well in a tin for at least a week (if nobody know it's there)! It also freezes well. Feel free to substitute your favorite flavor of jam. The strudel can also be filled with a savory filling such as mushroom and be used as an hors d'oeuvre.*

178

 ANDEL BREAD

4 eggs
1 C sugar
1 C canola oil
2½ heaping cups flour
1 tsp baking powder

Pinch salt
1 tsp vanilla
1 C walnuts or almonds,
coarsely broken or chopped
1 C mini-chocolate chips (optional)

Beat eggs and sugar together. Add oil and mix well. Add remaining ingredients in order given. Add optional ingredients, if desired. Mound batter into three long strips on each of two ungreased cookie sheets. Bake at 350° for approximately 20 minutes, or until golden. Remove from oven and slice and turn slices over onto sides. Put back into oven and bake another 5 minutes or until slices are slightly toasted.

Yield: 8 to 9 dozen pieces

Hint: This recipe is one the recipes I am best known for. A family friend invites my family to his house in New Hampshire every summer with the stipulation that I bake him a month's supply of mandel bread. My mother-in-law could survive on this; it is her favorite food! Try it with a cup of tea; you'll get hooked on it, too. It will keep well in a tin for up to 2 weeks.

 &M COOKIES

½ C butter or margarine
½ C brown sugar
¼ C granulated sugar
1 egg
½ tsp vanilla

¼ tsp water
1 heaping C flour
½ tsp baking soda
½ tsp salt
¾ C M&M's

Cream butter or margarine, both sugars, egg, vanilla and water until fluffy. Add remaining ingredients. Drop by teaspoonful onto ungreased cookie sheets. Bake at 375° for 10 to 12 minutes. Cool on wire rack.

Hint: I always double this recipe because they are eaten so fast! People of all ages love them. Now that there are different colored M&M's for every holiday, you can have color-coordinated cookies!

IANT CHOCOLATE CHIP COOKIE

1 C butter or margarine, softened
¾ C granulated sugar
¾ C brown sugar
1 tsp vanilla
2 eggs

2¼ C flour, sifted
1 tsp baking soda
½ tsp salt
2 C (12 oz pkg) chocolate chips
1 C walnuts, chopped (optional)

Cream butter or margarine, both sugars and vanilla until fluffy. Add eggs and remaining ingredients. Spread on a 14 or 15-inch greased pizza pan. Bake at 375° for 16 to 20 minutes, or until golden.

Hint: This makes a great birthday cake for those who prefer cookies to cake. Just write your message on the cookie. On Valentine's Day or someone's birthday, bake in a heart-shaped pan. It's a great way of saying "I love you!".

ICE KRISPIE CHOCOLATE CHIP COOKIES

1¼ C flour
½ tsp baking soda
¼ tsp salt
½ C butter or margarine
1 C sugar

1 egg
1 tsp vanilla
2 C Rice Krispies
1 C chocolate chips
1 C raisins

Combine first three ingredients and set aside. Cream butter or margarine and sugar until fluffy. Add egg and vanilla and beat until creamy. Blend in flour mixture. Fold in Rice Krispies, chocolate chips and raisins. Drop onto greased cookie sheet. Bake at 350° for 12 to 15 minutes.

Hint: These are similar to chocolate chip cookies, with the addition of a nutritional bonus.

179

180

PEANUT BUTTER MARBLE BARS

½ C crunchy peanut butter	1 C flour
⅓ C butter or margarine, softened	1 tsp baking powder
¾ C light brown sugar, packed	¼ tsp salt
¾ C granulated sugar	2 C (12 oz pkg) semi-sweet
2 eggs	chocolate chips
2 tsp vanilla	

Cream peanut butter, butter or margarine and both sugars in a large mixing bowl until light and fluffy. Add eggs and vanilla; beat well. In a separate bowl, combine flour, baking powder and salt; blend into peanut butter mixture. Spread batter in a greased 15½"x10½"x1" pan. Sprinkle chocolate chips evenly over top. Bake at 350° for 5 minutes. Remove from oven. Use a spatula or knife to swirl chips through batter for a marbled effect. Return to oven and bake at 350° for 13 to 14 minutes or until lightly browned. Cool completely in pan. Cut into bars.

Hint: These are a family favorite! They ship well, and are therefore good for college and camp care packages.

Index

Index

Index

Index

Index

Index

Index

Index

Index

4 Easy Ways to Order Additional Copies of
So Easy, So Delicious or *From Ellie's Kitchen To Yours*

Mail:
Denell Press
34 Crestwood Dr
Framingham, MA 01701

Phone:
(508) 620-1009

Fax:
(508) 620-1009

E-mail:
denellpress@verizon.net

		Quantity	Amount
So Easy, So Delicious	$16.95 each x		$
From Ellie's Kitchen To Yours	$18.95 each x		$
5% sales tax if delivered in MA			$
Gift wrap with enclosure card	$2.00 each x		$
Shipping for first book		1 @	$ 3.00
Shipping for each additional book	$1.00 each x		$
		Total	$

Method of payment:

☐ Check for $ _____ made payable to "Denell Press"

☐ VISA ☐ Mastercard   Credit card expires (mo./yr.) ___ ___ / ___ ___   CVV code: |___|___|___| (3 digit)

Credit card number: |___|___|___|___|___|___|___|___|___|___|___|___|___|___|___|___|

_____
Signature

Ordered by:

_____
Name

_____
Address

_____
City   State   Zip

_____
Evening Phone (in case we have questions)

Ship to: (if different than "ordered by")

_____
Name

_____
Address

_____
City   State   Zip

Delivery: ☐ To arrive within approximately 2 weeks
                   ☐ To arrive by _____

Other:

• For a personalized autographed copy,
  include the first name of recipient _____

• Inquire about quantity discounts for 5 or more books